Welcome to. . .

iPad for Beginners

The iPad is certainly one of the most intriguing products to have been released in recent times, and the excitement surrounding it is not unfounded. Allowing you to have extreme portability while still being able to do an incredible amount of day-to-day tasks, the iPad acts as a movable media hub, games console and much more, all alongside one of the most user-friendly and dynamic interfaces seen in a long time. It potentially changes the way we have being going about our lives for the last few years. Once you have your eager hands on this revolutionary device, you now need to find your way around it, and that can take a little getting used to. From using email, downloading apps and media, all the way to using word processing, **iPad for Beginners** ditches the jargon and shows you everything you need to know to set up your iPad and get started. Through easy to follow, step-by-step tutorials and features, we'll show you how to make the most out of this incredible piece of hardware, as well as pointing you in the direction of the essential apps you should download straight away. Welcome to the new wave of technology. Let's get started.

iPad for Beginners

Imagine Publishing Ltd
Richmond House
33 Richmond Hill
Bournemouth
Dorset BH2 6EZ
☎ +44 (0) 1202 586200
Website: www.imagine-publishing.co.uk

Editor-In-Chief
Aaron Asadi

Production Editor
Amy Squibb

Design
Danielle Dixon

Printed by
William Gibbons, 26 Planetary Road, Willenhall, West Midlands, WV13 3XT

Distributed in the UK & Eire by
Imagine Publishing Ltd, www.imagineshop.co.uk. Tel 01202 586200

Distributed in Australia by
Gordon & Gotch, Equinox Centre, 18 Rodborough Road, Frenchs Forest,
NSW 2086. Tel + 61 2 9972 8800

Distributed in the Rest of the World by
Marketforce, Blue Fin Building, 110 Southwark Street, London, SE1 0SU.

IMAGINE
PUBLISHING

Contents

Feature
132 100 essential apps
The must-have apps you simply have to download today

Feature

08 **First look at the iPad**
Get to know your iPad and how to use it effectively

Setting up

20 How to install iTunes
22 An overview of the iTunes interface
24 How to activate & register a new iPad
26 Sync email, contacts and bookmarks
28 Sync your music collection
29 Sync movies onto your iPad
30 Copy TV shows to your iPad
31 Sync podcasts onto your iPad
32 Learn how to sync books
33 Sync photos on your iPad
34 How to use iPad Settings
36 How to set up Wi-Fi
37 How to set up 3G
38 Access email on your iPad
40 Change Wallpaper on your iPad

Getting started

44 Moving icons and using folders
46 Work with multiple pages in Safari
48 Get the most from bookmarks on the iPad
50 Change the default search engine
52 Organising emails
54 How to work with attachments
56 Set the default calendar
58 Add an Event in Calendar
60 Add a contact
62 Creating, sending and receiving contacts
64 Use the iPad's Notes app
66 Save a bookmark in Maps
68 Get directions using Maps
70 Send and receive locations with Maps
72 Access video content via the YouTube app
74 Use the camera connection kit

76 Create a slideshow on the iPad
78 Set up a photo frame using your iPad
80 Get the most out of iPad videos
82 Easily create a song playlist using the iPod app
84 Use iTunes on the iPad
86 Use iTunes to get music
88 Use iTunes to get movies
90 Use iTunes to get television programmes
92 Create and save Genius playlists on your iPad
94 Use the App Store on your iPad

Find your way around the iPad hardware on page 8

"Learn how to get the most out of the iPad's apps from YouTube to iBooks and more"

96   Download iBooks from the App Store
98   Purchase an iBook
100   Getting to know iBooks
102   Creating Bookmarks in iBooks

The next step

106   Get to grips with Pages
108   Create spreadsheets with Numbers
110   Perform your presentations in style with Keynote
112   Use Dropbox to transfer files

114   Using the Voice Memos for iPad app
116   Stream content with AirPlay
118   Print from your iPad with AirPrint
120   Stream video directly to your iPad with Air Video
122   Get things done using Taska
124   Download and read eBooks using Kindle
126   Make your voice heard using Twitter
128   Using the Facebook app

Essential apps

132   100 essential apps
      The must-have apps everyone should download right away

App reviews:
The Elements: for UK and Ireland   140
Liquid Comics: Ramayan 3392AD, V1   141
Brushes iPad Edition   142
Epic Citadel   143
MaxJournal   144
Good Food Healthy Recipes for iPad   145
Tappy Memories   145
Chain Link HD   146

Grand Theft Auto: Chinatown Wars   147
Filterstorm 2   148
Faceover   149
Colors Pro   149
BBC News   150
USA Today   151
Drum Meister Grand   152
Red Bull BPM HD Player   152
Note Goal Pro   153
studio.HD   153
iFitness HD   154
Sky Sports News   155
CoPilot Live HD Europe   156
Urbanspoon   157
Wikihood for iPad   157
Air Display   158
Air Sketch   159
Atomic Web Browser   159
PocketMoney   160
Alarm Clock HD Free   161
IM+ Pro   162
Tweets   163
Dual Viewer For Facebook   163
NASA App   164
MathBoard   164
The World Factbook for iPad   165
WorldBook XL   165

Troubleshooting

168   Your problems solved
      All your questions answered

Wi-Fi signal strength
This symbol lets you know the signal strength it is receiving.

Available with or without 3G
If you want to use your iPad away from a Wi-Fi signal, you'll need the 3G model.

16, 32 or 64GB
The iPad comes in various storage sizes – the 16GB is cheapest.

10:15
Thursday, January 13

First look at the iPad

Let's explore the iPad's basic features

The iPad is unlike any computer you've ever put your hands on. For one thing, there's no intermediary between you and what you're trying to do; on a regular computer, you have to learn to manipulate a pointing device like a mouse or trackpad to move a cursor on the screen so you can achieve what you need to do. On the iPad, you're already an expert manipulator since you just use your fingers directly on the screen to move and affect what you see. If you know how to point, you know how to use an iPad, and that's the truly exciting thing

about this device: it makes personal computing truly personal.

But despite its obvious friendliness, it's still a remarkably complex piece of hardware and you'll need to know a little about what makes the iPad tick: how you turn it on, for instance, what's the function of its few buttons, and what about all the other controls embedded in the software itself? How can you use its many features to the fullest?

We will endeavour to show you all this over the next few pages, helping you feel comfortable with the device so you can hit the ground running in no time at all.

The volume control
Quickly control your sound with the buttons on the right.

Battery level indicator
You can visually see how much power your iPad has left here.

The mute switch
To kill the sound, just slide this switch.

The on/off switch
Turn your iPad on or off by holding the top-right button.

The screen (9.7" diagonal, with a resolution of 1024 x 768)
The iPad's high-res, LED-backlit screen is certainly impressive graphically for a tablet.

The speaker grille
The speaker is located here, and it does a great job for a small device.

The home button
This button takes you to the previous app launch screen.

The dock connector to sync and/or recharge
This is where you plug in your lead to sync or charge the iPad.

Browsing

As soon as you've connected to your local wireless network, the iPad is ready to be an internet browsing device. In fact, when Apple's engineers were first experimenting with touchscreen devices, the original idea was a tablet designed for web browsing. As a result, going online is a very polished experience and a joy to use. Like all other applications on the iPad, tapping on the Safari icon fills the screen with that program's content, removing any other distractions from view. You can then browse the web with your fingers. If you're familiar with Safari on your Mac or PC, you'll feel right at home – there's even a Google search field, top right of the screen. Tapping on it increases its size and reveals the keyboard so you can type what you're looking for. The same applies for the address field if you know exactly where you want to go.

If you're a MobileMe subscriber, you can sync your Mac's bookmarks straight to your iPad, right down to the Bookmark Bar.

Navigating a webpage is easy; you flick your finger up, down, left or right to see other parts of the page. If you want to focus on a specific section, double-tap on it for it to zoom in and fill the screen.

There are other browsers on the App Store, such as Opera Mini and Atomic, so have a browse to see if one suits your needs better than Safari.

Communication

Browsing the web isn't the only thing you need to do online. For one thing, you need to check your emails and the iPad's got you covered there as well, thanks to the Mail application. With it, you can setup as many accounts as you need. Just like Mail on your Mac, you have a universal inbox where all your messages, irrespective of which address they were sent to, can be accessed, read and replied to. You can also organise your messages in threads, making it easier to keep track of a conversation over time.

When it comes to social networking, you can either make use of Safari – aside from its games, Facebook works very well in the iPad's web browser (the games don't work because they rely on Adobe's Flash platform, which isn't compatible with the iPad, iPhone or iPod touch) – or look for dedicated programs available through the App Store. The program called Twitter is a good example of an original design to help you check your timeline easily via your iPad.

Other applications, like Skype, are also available but are designed with the iPhone in mind, meaning their interface isn't optimised for the iPad's larger screen size – although they work absolutely fine for text chat and voice calls.

Photos

If you see images on the web you'd like to keep, you can easily save them to your Photos application by tapping and holding on one and choosing 'Save Image' from the popover menu. But that's not the only use of that particular program. Thanks to iTunes on your Mac, you can transfer some or all of your images from your iPhoto or Aperture library straight to your iPad.

You can also dispense with a bigger computer entirely by getting the iPad Camera Connection Kit and transfer photos and videos from any compatible digital stills camera (including an iPhone or iPod touch) straight to your iPad library.

Once there, you can browse through them, post them online to your MobileMe account or send them via email to friends and family. If you want to upload them to Facebook or Flickr for example, you can do this straight from their own dedicated applications, which you can download for free from the App Store. Although just like Skype, they're designed for the smaller members of the iOS family, but they'll still work on the iPad.

First Steps

Getting acquainted with your iPad

Turn on
When an iPad's screen is off, your device is either asleep or shut down...

01. To turn it back on or wake it up, you have two options: you can either press the on/off button, top right of the device...

02. Alternatively, pressing the home button will also work to bring your iPad back to life.

Sleep mode
Putting your iPad to sleep is something you'll find yourself doing quite often.

01. You need to make use of one of your iPad's few physical buttons for this, namely the one top right of the device.

02. Press and release it once for the screen to go dark and become unresponsive to any touch inputs.

Turn off
Most of the time, you'll keep the iPad on, but asleep. To shut down, do the following:

01. Press and hold on its on/off button for up to five seconds. The screen will dim and a red slider will appear.

02. Slide that red button from left to right to confirm that you wish to shut the iPad down.

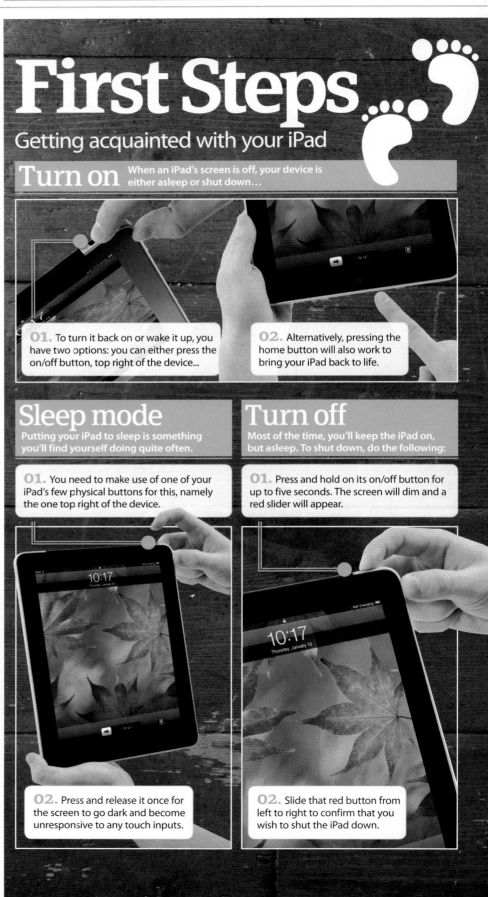

Change volume
Depending on what you're doing, you can change the volume is various ways...

01. Use the physical buttons, top of the iPad's right edge. The top one increases the volume and the bottom one lowers it.

02. If you're watching a movie or listen to music, you'll find a slider on the screen to achieve the same result.

Rotation lock
You may wish to stop the screen from rotating each time you change position. Here's how:

01. Double-tap on the home button to reveal a list of currently running apps. Slide that list to the left.

02. You'll find another volume control, bottom right. The rotation lock button is located bottom left of the screen.

Brightness
If the screen is too light or dark for your tastes, you can alter it in a couple of ways:

01. Tap on the Settings app and select the 'Brightness & Wallpaper' menu. Use the slider to lower or raise the brightness.

02. Double-click the home button and slide the new bar of icons to the left. You'll find a brightness slider there as well.

Unlock
Once you've woken your iPad up, you'll be graced with its Lock Screen. What next?

01. To gain access to your device, use the slider at the bottom to unlock your screen.

02. If you have set a password, you'll have to type it in before you can proceed any further.

Mute
To mute the volume, you have two options based on the iPad's physical buttons:

01. There's a switch above the volume controls; slide it down to mute your iPad.

02. You can also press and hold the volume down button. After a couple of seconds, your iPad will be muted.

Charging
Recharging the iPad is a simple matter:

01. Unless your computer is recent enough, there won't be enough power from its USB port to charge the iPad.

02. For a faster, more efficient charge, it's best to use the bundled power adapter instead.

Syncing
To back up or transfer files, you need to sync...

01. Use the bundled cable to connect your iPad via one of your computer's USB ports.

For more info
Go to page 24 for more on syncing the iPad.

02. It will launch iTunes and the backup and syncing process will be totally automatic.

Hardware

Music

It wouldn't be an Apple device if it didn't let you listen to your music, but although iTunes is responsible for almost everything media-related on your Mac, the iPad has broken those features into multiple applications designed for specific purposes. For instance, you can purchase new music using the iTunes application, but if you want to listen to albums you currently own, then you have to use the iPod software instead. From there, you gain access to your songs, podcasts and audiobooks. If you want to watch a music video however, you'll need to take a trip to the Videos application.

But iTunes isn't the only way you can listen to music on your iPad. There are other programs that let you stream songs directly from the internet and just like the iPod application, they can be used to listen to music in the background while you work in another program on your iPad. If you're in the UK, make sure you check out Spotify, while US readers should take a look at Pandora.

Watching

Although it's no substitute for your widescreen television, when you're away from your couch, the iPad makes for a surprisingly good TV. Due to its size, it's much better than an iPhone or iPod touch and its built-in speaker is good enough to allow the device to be shared, but what can you watch on it? Well, anything you've bought or rented from the iTunes Store will work on your iPad: you can transfer movies, TV shows, podcasts and music videos and they'll all play flawlessly on your portable device.

"Videos all play flawlessly on your portable device"

You could also convert your existing DVD collection into iTunes-compatible files but in order to achieve this, you'd need programs like HandBrake which are designed to transform your films and episodes into compatible files ready for you to enjoy on your iPad. This can be a time-consuming process, so if you'd rather not have to deal with any of this and you happen to own an Elgato Netstream device which is connected to your network, you can purchase the EyeTV application and watch live TV straight from your iPad, anywhere in your house, as long as you're within range of your wireless signal.

Entertainment

There's been a lot of talk about the iPad (and any other iOS device) not being compatible with Adobe's Flash, but this is actually less of a problem than you might think. For one thing, although you won't be able to go to www.youtube.com and watch videos via the Safari web browser, there's a dedicated YouTube application which enables you to do just that. You can watch clips, comment on them, and do pretty much everything you'd expect. Other video-sharing sites, like Vimeo, are getting on the iOS-friendly bandwagon and offer iPad-compatible versions of their videos, so you can watch those straight from your web browser.

But being entertained is much more than just passively watching something on the screen; you can also use your iPad to read the latest bestseller or enjoy a timeless classic. The two major programs that allow you to do this are Apple's own iBooks and Amazon's Kindle. Both are also compatible with the iPod and iPhone so you can stop reading on the iPad and carry on with another device if you'd like. That compatibility doesn't extend to your Mac for the iBooks though, but it does for the Kindle. Not all titles are available in digital form yet, but there's enough there to keep you busy for days.

Games

When it comes to games, you'll be spoilt for choice. There are so many available to download, both free or paid-for that you can spend hours getting immersed in an adventure story (thank goodness for the iPad's excellent battery life), or just use it to while away a few minutes of your time.

The obvious choices are there, like arcade-type games such as *The Incident* and *Fruit Ninja HD*, to adventure games like *Hero of Sparta 2* and *Max*, to strategy games like *Cut the Rope* and *Angry Birds* or role-playing adventures like *Aralon* or *Galaxy on Fire 2*. There's even a version of *Farmville*.

But none of these offer anything new from what you could achieve on a regular computer. What sets the iPad apart from other platforms is that its screen is large enough that it can be easily viewed by multiple people at the same time. As a result, it's become a natural digital alternative to board games, making playing on a computer a much more social experience with people in the same room as you, just like the good old days. Make sure you check out titles like WarChess, Carcassonne, Scrabble, Monopoly and the Game of Life. Whatever your tastes, though, the iPad has it covered.

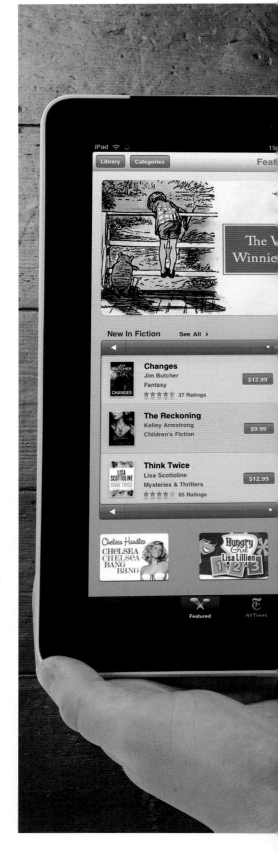

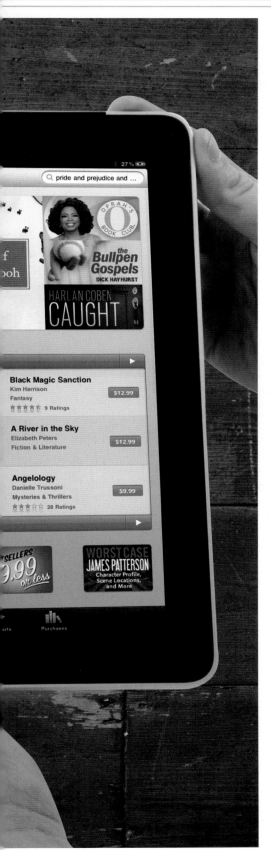

iTunes
The desktop software explored

What is iTunes?

A It's a program designed by Apple and the original purpose was to transfer your CD collection onto your Mac, catalogue your songs and transfer them to a compatible MP3 player. A lot's changed since these humble days.

Why do I need it?

A Because iTunes evolved over the years to accommodate more than music – from movies, TV shows, podcasts and more. Now it's the most popular way to transfer anything to your iPad.

Why is it not included on a CD?

A Apple now assumes that broadband is ubiquitous and that way, the company can make sure that you'll be using the very latest version available as opposed to one that could have been released months previously.

How do I cancel the sync?

A When your iPad is connected to iTunes, its screen informs you not to disconnect it from your computer. However, there's a slider at the bottom which you can use to cancel the sync should you need to. Your iPad will not be fully backed up if you do this, however.

Is there anything else I need to do?

A Not really. The process is completely automatic and if you don't want to get any more involved in the process, you don't have to. Once the sync is complete, you can unplug your device and carry on using it.

Can I control what's on my iPad?

A Absolutely. Look down iTunes' sidebar until you find the Devices section. Click on your iPad and

Where can I get it?

A Point your browser towards **www.itunes.com** and click on the 'Download iTunes' button, somewhere on the page (it's currently on the right, near the top, but that could change).

It's installed. Now what?

A Double-click on its icon to open it and agree to the licence agreement. You can convert your music CDs to iPad-compatible files or purchase new songs, movies and shows from the iTunes Store. But none of this is compulsory.

What happens when I connect my iPad to my computer?

A iTunes will take over your iPad and you will be asked not to disconnect it while the syncing process is taking place. Your iPad's data will be backed up and your media will be synchronised between both devices.

the main part of the interface will let you choose which songs, films, podcasts, applications and so on you'd like to transfer over.

What about my emails, calendars and contacts?

A That's all possible as well from the same section in iTunes as mentioned above. You can find all the details and choose which calendars, contacts and emails you'd like to import from the Info section.

Hardware

"Chances are someone may already have designed a great solution that fits your exact needs"

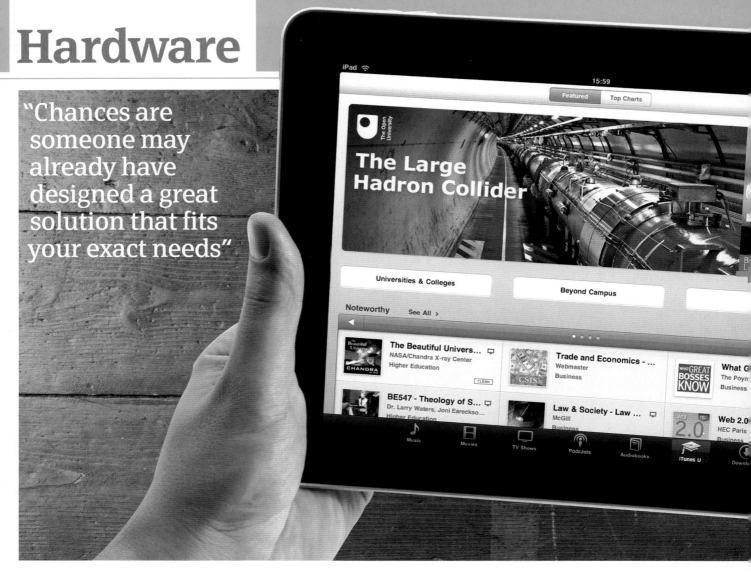

Office work

The iPad isn't just a device to browse the web, watch videos and play games however. Many people classify it as just a media consumption device, but it's in fact a very powerful machine capable of doing almost anything a regular computer can. It comes with a Notes program which you can use to jot down a few ideas, lists, or even the beginning of a draft letter. That application syncs with your emails and you can access those documents in your Mac's Mail program, which is very convenient and enables you to work between the two systems.

But the iPad can go a lot further than this. For one thing, the iWork suite is available for it as a separate purchase. You won't obviously get all the features you've grown accustomed to with the Mac's versions, but for a first attempt at creating a business suite that's controlled by touch, it's remarkable what you can do with them and you'll be designing newsletters, filling in spreadsheets and creating presentations in next to no time.

If you need compatibility with Microsoft Word and iWork's conversion layer isn't good enough, take a look at Byte²'s Office² HD. It's not as attractive as the iWork suite, but it lets you create native Word (both .doc and .docx) and Excel (.xls) documents on your iPad for a very reasonable price.

Productivity

As for other productivity programs, Calendar stores all your appointments and syncs with iCal on your Mac – as long as you've got a MobileMe subscription. The same applies for the Contacts app, even preserving all your groups so you'll feel right at home on your new machine.

Surprisingly, unlike the iPod touch or iPhone, the iPad doesn't come with a calculator, but this can be easily remedied with a short visit to the App Store. Just type on "Calculator" in the search field to find enough free and paid options to satisfy your needs.

Another feature missing from the iPad is any possibility of using it like an external drive, but the fantastic advantage of the iPad and any device powered by the iOS software is the huge number of developers working on it. As a result, someone's come up with a way of achieving just that thanks to an application called 'USB Disk Pro for iPad' (a free version is also available under the title of 'USB Disk for iPad') so you can easily use your iPad like an external portable hard drive.

Chances are, whatever it is you're looking for, someone may already have designed a solution that fits your exact needs.

Creative apps

That's exactly the case with graphic design applications. Adobe, maker of the mighty Photoshop, has only dipped its toes in the iPad, but other, smaller developers have jumped at the opportunity that this new platform offers them and there's a wealth of programs that allow you to design with your fingers anything you used to need a mouse or a graphic tablet for in the past.

App Store FAQ

A vital part of the iPad explained

What's all this talk about apps? Do I need them?

A Apps, or applications, are programs that run on a computer, like your browser or word processor. They increase your device's functionality and you should definitely browse through them to see if there's anything you might find crucial to your life on the iPad.

Where do I get those apps?

A Straight from the App Store, which you can access from iTunes itself. You might find some websites showcasing various programs, but you can only purchase and download them from iTunes.

What if I'm just browsing? Can I find stuff easily?

A Of course: the App Store is really designed to help you buy programs. As a result, you can look through various lists like top sellers, top free apps, staff recommendations, and so on.

Is there any trial software I can use?

A Not as such, but many developers have 'lite' or 'free' versions of their applications. These offer limited functionality or a few sample levels if it's a game. If you like what you see, you can then purchase the full program and delete the lite copy.

How do I find what I want?

A With over 60,000 apps designed specifically for the iPad, you may feel that you may never find the exact program you need. Try using the search field to narrow down the results.

Can I only get them from my computer?

A No: there's a program called 'App Store' on your iPad. From there, you can gain access to the entire store as well, although you will need to be within range of a Wi-Fi network, unless of course you own an 3G-capable iPad.

It's all a bit of a jumble; can I narrow my search down?

A The App Store is broken into 20 categories, each with its own top sellers list. You can narrow your search by focusing on a single category.

Why can't I comment on a program I'm looking at?

A In order to limit bogus reviews or overly negative or positive comments from people who've never used the program, Apple links your reviews to your account. The company can therefore check if you own the app and if you don't, you can only read, not contribute.

How can I ask questions or get help from the developer?

A At the bottom of every app description is a link to the developer's own website. More often than not, you'll find a help forum or contact email address there which you can use to write to the developer or company and get the help you need.

Why does my App Store icon have red numbers on it?

A These badges are there to show you that some of the programs you've acquired have been updated and that you can get those new versions for free directly from the App Store's Updates section on your iPad (or computer).

"The iPad is a very powerful machine capable of doing almost anything a computer can"

The beauty of the iPad is that these programs are so cheap compared to those you'd find on a Mac or PC, that trying some out isn't as financially crippling as it can be on other platforms.

You're bound to find the right program that matches your abilities. If you're professionally inclined, have a look at SketchBook Pro, Freeform or Brushes. If you're looking for programs that help you transform pictures into visually stunning works of art, explore Artist's Touch or the PhotoArtistaHD series of applications. If you fancy more specific effects, consider TypeDrawing or Glow Painter Pro HD. Those of you missing iPhoto's adjustment tools should purchase TouchUp, and your children (or the child inside you) will love Drawing Pad.

Hardware

Kids

The iPad is an amazing learning tool no matter what your age is; there's even a dedicated section called "Apps for Kids" in the App Store where you can get interactive books like *Winnie the Pooh* or *The Cat in the Hat*, programs that teach you how to read and write or even understand the world around you, help you play music, draw, … pretty much anything you can imagine.

Older children haven't been left out either: MathBoard is a fantastic program designed to help you perfect your algebra. You can even set which calculations to work on and how difficult they should be. There are also things to keep them entertained such as wordsearch apps like WordSeek HD and much more.

If you're interested in space, you can learn everything you need to know thanks to programs like Solar Walk or Solar System for iPad, and the little ones can keep up with their older siblings with iLearn Solar System HD. If it's dinosaurs you're after, check out Ultimate Dinopedia, and if you want to explore all the elements that make up our universe, be sure to look for The Elements - there's even a British edition with UK English spelling.

Maps

All of the above can be achieved whether you own a Wi-Fi only-iPad or one capable of connecting to a 3G network (ie, one that hooks up to a mobile phone network and hence gets you online wherever you have coverage – for a price). If you've decided to invest in a 3G-capable iPad, the capabilities of your machine are greatly extended since you'll be able to browse, check you emails or even play online games wherever you might be.

There's also the added advantage of being able to use the Maps application to help you navigate to your desired location. This application will even show you areas to avoid due to traffic jams or dense circulation. But even if you decided to stick to the Wi-Fi-only version, you should definitely give Maps a try. You may get tired of hearing how "magical" the iPad is, but it's undeniable how truly amazing it is to be able to scroll through a map and effortlessly zoom in and out of a location using your fingers alone. The program is incredibly responsive and the only limitation you'll experience will be due to your internet's bandwidth. It illustrates just how wonderful using this device truly is. There are also other map apps available, so check out the App Store to find one that suits you.

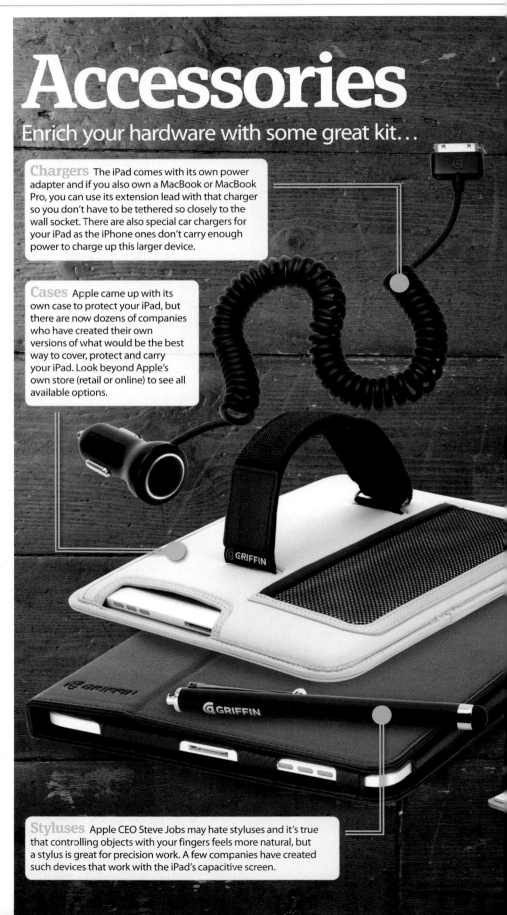

Accessories
Enrich your hardware with some great kit…

Chargers The iPad comes with its own power adapter and if you also own a MacBook or MacBook Pro, you can use its extension lead with that charger so you don't have to be tethered so closely to the wall socket. There are also special car chargers for your iPad as the iPhone ones don't carry enough power to charge up this larger device.

Cases Apple came up with its own case to protect your iPad, but there are now dozens of companies who have created their own versions of what would be the best way to cover, protect and carry your iPad. Look beyond Apple's own store (retail or online) to see all available options.

Styluses Apple CEO Steve Jobs may hate styluses and it's true that controlling objects with your fingers feels more natural, but a stylus is great for precision work. A few companies have created such devices that work with the iPad's capacitive screen.

Camera Connection Kit Your iPad may be too bulky a device to take pictures with, but that doesn't mean it can't be an ideal companion to your digital camera: equipped with a Camera Connection Kit, you can plug in your camera via the dock connector and transfer all your images onto your iPad.

TV connectors Wouldn't it be great if you could watch all that media stored on your iPad directly on your widescreen TV? If you had an Apple TV, you could use AirPlay, but failing that, you can get video cables to achieve a similar result.

Headphones Strange as it may seem, even though the iPad is designed for you to enjoy music, films and shows with, it doesn't actually come with headphones. But you're not limited to Apple's own version; you can choose any type that connects via a 3.5mm stereo mini-jack or even a Bluetooth set.

Protective films Even if you prefer your iPad to be without a case, you should consider a film around its most important part: the screen. Some high quality ones not only protect it from accidental scratches, they actually make it easier to clean and fingerprints don't stick as easily as they would on a bare piece of glass.

Docks and keyboards Apple makes a dock to recharge your iPad while keeping it upright. You can then use an external keyboard, which can be faster than typing on glass. Any Bluetooth one would work or even USB keyboards if you hook it up via the Camera Connection Kit.

Speakers The iPad's mono speaker may be surprisingly good for an item of its size, but it's really not sufficient to enjoy your media to its fullest. Thankfully, there are many external speakers available to improve the experience. They either connect via its mini-jack, the dock connector or even wirelessly via Bluetooth.

Setting up

Bring your iPad to life with these easy to follow tips to get you up and running

20 How to install iTunes
Download iTunes to your Mac or PC

22 An overview of the iTunes interface
Get to know this vital software

24 How to activate & register a new iPad
Get your iPad up and running

26 Sync email, contacts and bookmarks
Backup your important details

28 Sync your music collection
Move music from your computer to your iPad

29 Sync movies onto your iPad
Copy films from your desktop to your tablet

30 Copy TV shows to your iPad
Shift your favourite programmes from your Mac or PC to your iPad

31 Sync podcasts onto your iPad
Move podcasts from computer to iPad

32 Learn how to sync books
Get previously purchased eBooks onto your iPad

33 Sync photos on your iPad
Store your photos on your device

34 How to use iPad Settings
Set up your iPad up the way you want

36 How to set up Wi-Fi
Access the internet wirelessly

37 How to set up 3G
Get online wherever you are

38 Access email on your iPad
Stay connected by getting emails straight to your iPad

40 Change Wallpaper on your iPad
Customise your backdrop with ease

Step one
Install iTunes

Step two
Activate & register

Step three
Sync your info

Step four
Set up your iPad

How to install iTunes

Unlike most other devices, Apple's iPods, iPhones and iPads don't come with any installer CDs. In order to make your device work, you need to take a trip to the internet

Despite the fact that the iPad is a powerful computer in its own right, you cannot turn it on and start using it as soon as you unpack it. Just like the iPod touch and iPhone, it needs to hook up with your copy of iTunes on your Mac or PC before you can do anything else. The good news is that once you've connected it and your iPad is set up, you can choose never to perform that action again since you can get everything you need directly from the web. But you can't bypass this crucial first step.

To set up the iPad, you need the latest version of iTunes, namely 10.1 or above. So even if you already own a copy of iTunes, if it isn't recent, you may have to get online and update it before it'll recognise the iPad as a valid device.

Although slightly inconvenient, finding the installer program online and installing the software isn't too difficult, as we'll show you over the course of this tutorial.

"The iPad needs to hook up with iTunes before you can do anything else"

iTunes Installing iTunes on your Mac or PC

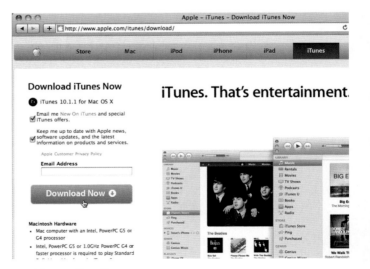

01 Get online
Your first step is to launch your favourite web browser and point it in the direction of **www.itunes.com**. The layout of the page changes regularly, but there will be a 'Download iTunes' button somewhere within it (currently, it's located in the top-right corner of the page).

02 Download now
This will lead you to the proper download page. Your browser will recognise the type of computer you're on so you won't be offered any choices that could lead to confusion. You'll see a single 'Download Now' button. Only enter your email if you want to receive promotional messages from Apple.

The iTunes Download page

What each part of the Download page does

Automatic detection
All modern browsers transmit what type of computer you are currently using and clever websites can take advantage of that information to only offer you the choices that match those criteria

Email notifications
By default, these two tick boxes are enabled, which means that you won't be able to download iTunes without typing in your email address first. If you'd rather stay anonymous, untick them

System requirements
If you're at all uncertain if your computer will be able to run the software, this section displays the necessary system requirements that match the machine you're currently running

Privacy Policy
If you're concerned about what Apple might do with the information you give them (namely, your email address, as requested on this page), you can check out its policy by clicking here

Knowledge base
Why can't Apple include a copy of iTunes with its products?
It would be more convenient at first glance for Apple to just bundle a CD with the packaging. After all, every other company does that. But the problem with this idea is that the software gets updated regularly, and that CD could be months old by the time it reaches you, meaning that you wouldn't be taking advantage of any updates or bug fixes that would have been made since then. Most people seldom update their software anyway, so since, rightly or wrongly, Apple assumes that its clients have broadband, this is its way of making sure you get the latest and greatest as soon as you get your iPad.

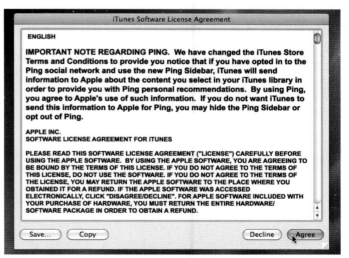

03 Installing
Once the download is complete, a new window will open up with a semi-transparent iTunes logo inside it. The 'Read Before You Install iTunes' document gives you the minimum requirements without which the program will not function. Double-click 'Install iTunes' to proceed.

04 Licence Agreement
Once iTunes has been installed, its icon should appear in your Dock or Desktop. If it hasn't you'll be able to locate it in your Applications or Program Files folder. The first time you double-click on it, you'll have to agree to the licence agreement. Agreeing grants you access to the software.

Setting up

An overview of the iTunes interface

iTunes has morphed from a program designed to look after your music library to one capable of storing any media you'd care to enjoy, all while being the gateway to Apple's online store

The first version of iTunes was released a decade ago, back on 9 January 2001. Apple had purchased Casady and Greene's SoundJam MP two years previously, realising that it had missed the boat with regards to the CD ripping and burning that was going on at the time. Back then, the iPod didn't even exist. Three years later, the iTunes Music Store was born, along with Apple's ambitions as an online entertainment retailer.

Today, you can't even start using your iPad without connecting it to your copy of iTunes first. Among its original duty of managing your growing media libraries, it's become the portal through which you can access everything you need for all your iOS devices (iPod Touch, iPhone and iPad), even down to upgrading their system software.

This tutorial is designed to help you understand where everything iPad-related can be found within the iTunes interface, with a particular emphasis on locating the apps you want in the iTunes Store.

"It's the portal through which you can access everything you need"

iTunes Getting to know the software

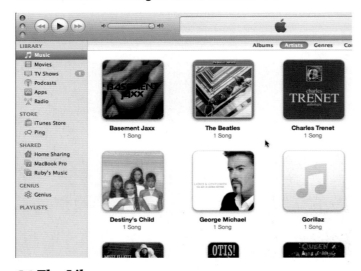

01 The Library
Your media is broken down by type, like music, films, television shows, podcasts, books and apps for your iOS devices, all of which you can acquire from the iTunes Store. The last one on the list, Radio, lets you listen to online radio stations for free.

02 The Store
To access Apple's online media store, move your cursor to the Store section in the Sidebar and click on iTunes Store. The front page is geared towards entertainment, showing you the latest and most popular songs and albums, films and TV shows (books can only be purchased from your iOS device).

Browsing the App Store
Helping you find the apps you need in seconds

Categories
Narrow down your search by browsing through a specific category. To access this menu, click on the small triangle to the right of 'App Store'

Search and find
If none of these are of any help, you can always use the good old-fashioned search field. Start typing and a list of options will appear for you to choose from

New & Noteworthy
Sometimes a recommendation is all you need, and the New & Noteworthy section shows you a selection of staff favourites that you may feel suit your exact needs

Top Charts
Looking at the bestselling apps can help you decide what to get. This one on the front page shows the top sellers irrespective of their category (categories also have their own charts)

Knowledge base
How do I choose what to add to my iPad?
By default, iTunes is designed to take care of that for you: even if you have more media than can fit in your iPad, it'll choose which ones to add, and which to leave behind. But if you'd like more control over the process, start by clicking on the iPad in the Devices section. From there, you'll have options in the various tabs to select which songs, films or apps you'd like to include. There are multiple ways of doing this, which will be explained in other parts of this book.

03 Finding the apps
To get to the App Store and start browsing for programs for your iPad, check out the menu bar, top of the main part of the iTunes interface, and click on App Store. Once there, you'll find two buttons at the top, one labelled iPhone, the other iPad. Click on iPad.

04 Connecting your iPad
After activating your iPad (see pages 24 and 25), it'll appear in the Sidebar under the Devices section. Click on its name and you'll gain access to your device. You can use that section to select which media to add and which apps to install, or just let iTunes add everything automatically.

How to activate & register a new iPad

Until registered and activated using iTunes, an iPad cannot be fully used.
Follow us over the next two pages as we explain how it's done

The iPad is a fully fledged computer with full access to the web, email, videos, hundreds of thousands of apps, and more. It's the perfect device for anyone new to computing, or for those looking for an efficient way to access the web around the home. However, as we've already said, the iPad does not fully work out of the box until the device is activated and registered using iTunes. This can be done by an Apple employee within an Apple store, but for anyone who buys the device online or in a typical retail store, a desktop computer or laptop will need to be used to get the iPad up and running.

Thankfully, activating and registering an iPad takes mere minutes. All that's needed is a Mac or PC with a working connection to the web and the latest version of iTunes, as we're about to explain…

"The iPad does not work out of the box until the device is activated and registered using iTunes"

iTunes Activating your iPad

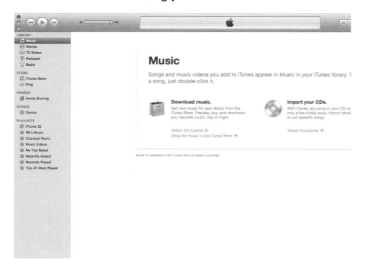

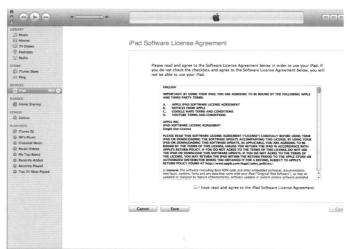

01 Turn on

Take your brand new iPad out of its box and turn it on by pressing the black button on top of the device. Next, turn on a PC or Mac and open iTunes. If you don't already have a copy installed, or you need to update to the latest version, it can be downloaded for free from **www.apple.com/itunes**.

02 Plug in and set up

Once iTunes has been opened, plug your iPad into the computer using the supplied USB cable. iTunes will automatically detect the device and launch the activation window. You'll need to read Apple's terms and conditions, so once you're happy click on the Accept button at the bottom of the page.

Discover the basics of syncing

Find your way around the Devices section of iTunes

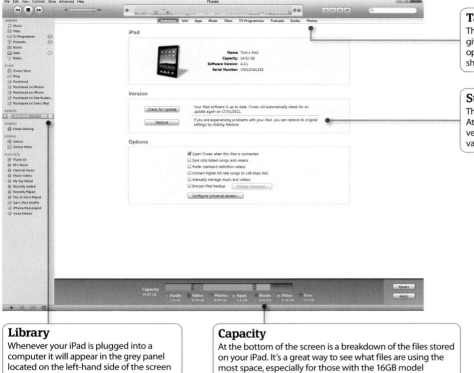

Tab buttons
The nine buttons at the top of the screen give you quick access to various syncing options, including apps, music, films, TV shows and photos

Summary
This window gives an overview of your iPad. At the top of the screen are the device's version number and serial. Below you'll find various options for syncing and backup

Library
Whenever your iPad is plugged into a computer it will appear in the grey panel located on the left-hand side of the screen

Capacity
At the bottom of the screen is a breakdown of the files stored on your iPad. It's a great way to see what files are using the most space, especially for those with the 16GB model

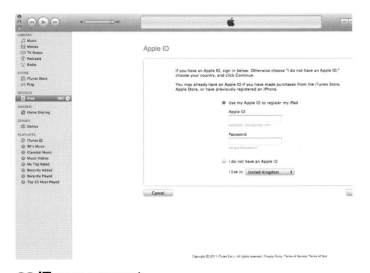

03 iTunes account
You'll be asked to log in using your iTunes account. Don't worry if you don't already have one as it's free to create a new account. Once complete, iTunes will ask if you would like to automatically sync applications, photos, music and videos.

04 Syncing
Click yes to automatically sync every picture, video and music track on the computer. If you're using a friend's machine or would rather choose which files to sync, deselect this option. Click OK and the activation process will complete. Congratulations, your iPad is now ready to use!

Setting up

Sync email, contacts and bookmarks

Never lose an email, contact or web browser bookmark by syncing all three through iTunes. Here's how easy it is…

Syncing through iTunes might seem like an inconvenience at times, but it's a really great way to ensure that you never lose any personal data, apps, files or documents. That's because every time your iPad is plugged into the computer and synced, every file is backed up on your desktop computer. As a result, if you require a new device or buy a second iPad you can sync it via iTunes and automatically copy every file into its correct place.

You may already be aware that music, movies, TV shows and apps are backed up on your computer with every sync, but did you also know that contacts, emails and bookmarks are also synced? It's a great timesaver when setting up a new device, removing the need to manually type every contact from your address book, setting up email accounts and browser bookmarks. Follow us over the next two pages as we explain how to properly sync these important files.

> ## "Syncing is a great way to ensure that you never lose any personal data"

iTunes Sync everything you need

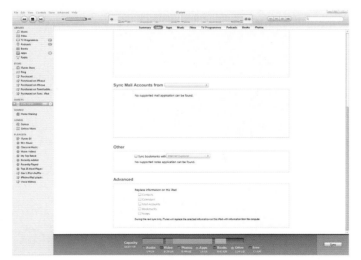

01 Email

iPad supports syncing to Mail and Outlook accounts. To sync either of these, plug your iPad into your computer, select it from the grey bar on the left in iTunes, then click on the Info tab. You'll find a Mail accounts button on this screen that enables you to sync an email account.

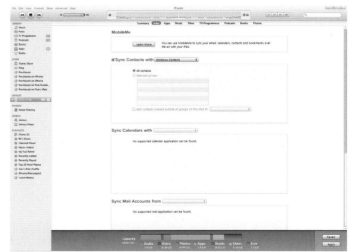

02 Contacts

The iPad can sync contacts with the Mac Address Book, Windows Contacts and Outlook. Simply sync your iPad with iTunes, select it from the left-hand side grey bar and click on the Info tab. Windows users need to check 'Sync contacts from'; Mac users can click on 'Sync Address Book contacts'.

Syncing contacts, mail and bookmarks

Everything you need to know about the iTunes Info pane

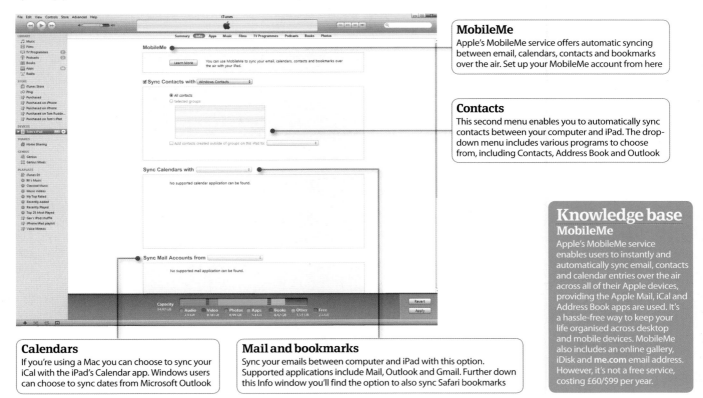

MobileMe
Apple's MobileMe service offers automatic syncing between email, calendars, contacts and bookmarks over the air. Set up your MobileMe account from here

Contacts
This second menu enables you to automatically sync contacts between your computer and iPad. The drop-down menu includes various programs to choose from, including Contacts, Address Book and Outlook

Calendars
If you're using a Mac you can choose to sync your iCal with the iPad's Calendar app. Windows users can choose to sync dates from Microsoft Outlook

Mail and bookmarks
Sync your emails between computer and iPad with this option. Supported applications include Mail, Outlook and Gmail. Further down this Info window you'll find the option to also sync Safari bookmarks

Knowledge base
MobileMe
Apple's MobileMe service enables users to instantly and automatically sync email, contacts and calendar entries over the air across all of their Apple devices, providing the Apple Mail, iCal and Address Book apps are used. It's a hassle-free way to keep your life organised across desktop and mobile devices. MobileMe also includes an online gallery, iDisk and **me.com** email address. However, it's not a free service, costing £60/$99 per year.

03 Bookmarks

It's possible to sync Safari bookmarks to the iPad. Simply sync the iPad with iTunes, select it from the grey bar on the left again and choose the Info tab. From there, scroll down the page and check Sync Safari Bookmarks. Click Apply and every bookmark will be synced to your iPad.

04 Sync Google contacts

Have a Google account? You can sync its contacts by selecting your iPad from the left-hand side grey bar in iTunes then clicking on the Info tab at the top of the screen. From there, select 'Sync address book contacts', then click 'Sync Google contacts' at the bottom of the list.

Sync your music collection

Here's how easy it is to sync your music collection from a computer to the iPad

It might not exactly be pocketable, but the iPad is easily Apple's best music player to date. Its 9.7-inch display makes it easy to browse the music library, album artwork looks gorgeous when viewed full-screen and the Library found in the desktop version makes a comeback, giving quick access to podcasts, audiobooks, genius mixes and more. We can say with confidence that the iPad is the most fun way to listen to music.

Getting music onto your iPad is a simple process, done entirely through iTunes. It's possible to sync tracks, albums or your entire music library. iTunes remembers your settings, so whenever your iPad is plugged into the computer it automatically syncs any new music tracks to the device. By spending just a few minutes setting up your music sync options, you'll never have to manually transfer tracks and albums again.

iTunes Get your music on your iPad

01 Import tunes

First, ensure you have music tracks in your iTunes Library. Simply drag MP3 files from your computer to the iTunes interface to add them.

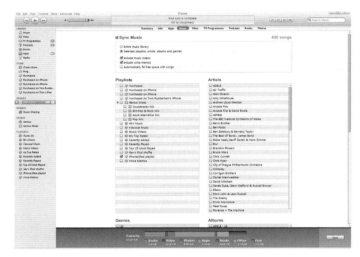

02 Get to your music

Turn on your iPad then plug it into your Mac or PC. Once iTunes has synced, click on your iPad from the Library window, then click the Music tab.

03 Choose what to sync

From here you can choose what to sync. Once you're happy with the selection, click the Apply/Sync button at the bottom of the screen.

04 Get playing

Once the syncing process has been completed, turn on your iPad and open the iPod app located in the dock at the bottom of the screen.

Sync movies onto your iPad

We explain how easy it is to copy movies from your desktop computer to an iPad

Movies look amazing on the iPad screen. Whether laying in bed or sitting on a train with the iPad in your hands, the display shows off movies with vivid clarity. It gets even better if the movie has been purchased or rented through the iTunes Store, as the iPad will display detailed information about the film and enable users to skip directly to a particular chapter with just one tap of the finger. For those with an Apple TV it's also possible to wirelessly stream any movie to the device from your iPad, enabling you to watch films on a high-definition TV and control the playback using the iPad's touch screen display, but more on that later.

In this tutorial we'll explain how easy it is to sync movies from your desktop computer to the iPad using iTunes. In next to no time you'll be up and running with a selection of great movies on your iPad.

iTunes Sync your movies to your iPad

01 Get ready
Ensure you have movies to sync in iTunes. Films can be purchased from the iTunes Store, or copied to your iTunes Library in MOV or MP4 format.

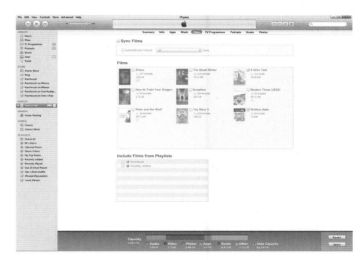

02 Select films
Connect your iPad and click on it in iTunes, then select the Films tab at the top of the screen. If unselected, check the top Sync Films button.

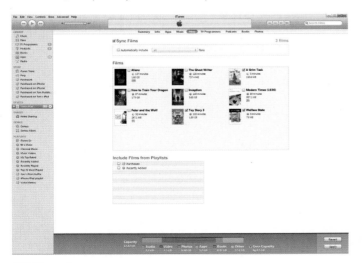

03 Sync!
Select the films that you wish to sync, but keep aware of the file sizes. Once you're happy, click the Apply/Sync button at the bottom of the screen.

04 Get watching
Once the films have copied you can watch them from the Videos app. If purchased from the Store, they will include chapters for easy navigation.

Copy TV shows to your iPad

The iPad's perfect for watching programmes on the go. Here's how to sync TV shows from a Mac/PC

With its relatively large 9.7-inch display and lengthy battery life, the iPad is pretty much the perfect portable television. Its screen is large enough to be easily viewed by more than one person and all images look fantastic on its colourful, high-resolution screen. For anyone who travels a lot, it's the perfect way to keep entertained on long journeys, and because the iPad is so portable you can continue watching wherever you are in your home.

Getting TV shows onto your iPad is a simple process. By opening the iTunes app you can purchase the latest episodes of your favourite show and download them directly to the device. Alternatively it's possible to sync all the shows on your desktop computer to the iPad by using the desktop version of iTunes. Follow us through this tutorial as we explain how easy it is to sync your TV shows in just four steps. You'll have all of your favourite TV programmes ready to watch on your iPad in no time.

iTunes Watch downloaded television shows on your iPad

01 The right place
Just in case, click on Movies and, if any TV shows are located there, right-click on them, choose 'Options' and select 'TV Shows' from the Media Kind menu.

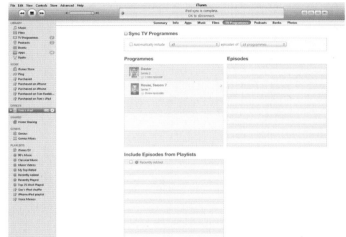

02 Plug and sync
Plug your iPad into the computer. Once it has synced, select it from the grey bar on the left. Next, click on TV Programmes at the top of the screen.

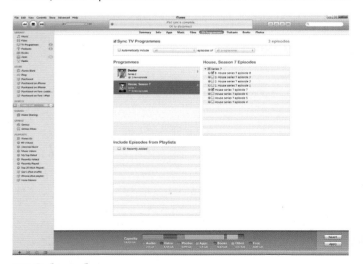

03 Select shows
If Sync TV Programmes isn't already checked, tick it to enable syncing. Once you're happy with the selection of TV shows, click the Apply/Sync button.

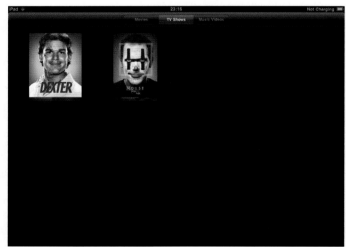

04 Get watching
You can view TV shows from the Videos app on your iPad. Simply open the app and you'll see a TV Shows button at the top of the screen.

Sync podcasts onto your iPad

Discover how to sync podcasts from your desktop computer to an iPad

Think of podcasts as individual radio shows without the music – some are a few minutes long, others hours in length, and they can be listened to from within the iPod app on your iPad. Once you've found a great podcast it's possible to subscribe to it from the iPad's iTunes app, enabling your desktop computer or iPad to automatically download the latest episodes as soon as they're available, ready for you to enjoy. With podcasts you can pick and choose the subjects that interest you, enabling you to skip the annoying adverts and subject matters that you normally sit through when listening to the radio.

In this tutorial we'll explain how to subscribe to podcasts and sync them between your desktop computer and iPad. It's a simple process done entirely through iTunes. Once you've subscribed to a handful of podcasts you'll find yourself with hours of free entertainment, and wondering how you ever lived without them.

iTunes Listen to podcasts on your iPad

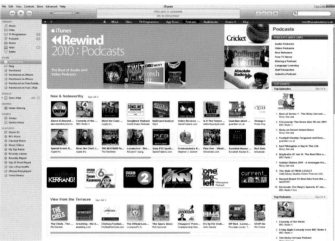

01 Download new podcasts
Open iTunes on your Mac or PC, click on the iTunes Store button then choose Podcasts from the menu at the top of the screen.

02 Plug and sync
Once you've got the podcasts, plug your iPad into your Mac/PC. Click your iPad from the grey side panel, then the Podcasts button at the top.

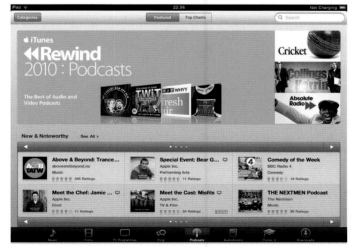

03 Syncing options
From the Podcasts window you can choose to sync individual podcasts, entire subscriptions or only the podcasts with new episodes available.

04 Podcasts on your iPad
You can play synced podcasts from the iPod app. To get podcasts without a Mac/PC, open the iTunes app on your iPad and you'll find a Podcasts button.

Learn how to sync books

Find out how to sync books with your iPad, and where to download the latest titles

Before the iPad was even announced, media pundits were declaring it to be the saviour of print media. Now that it's been in the hands of customers for a year, it's beginning to justify that claim, as the iPad is a fantastic device for reading books and magazines for a number of reasons. Its large 9.7-inch display makes reading text a joy, the vivid colour screen makes images look even better than their printed counterparts, its support for multimedia means videos and web links can be embedded in books, it's

possible to change the font and text size, look up words with a dictionary and easily control the brightness for when reading in a low-lit environment. The list goes on.

eBooks can either be synced from a desktop computer, purchased directly from Apple's iBooks app or from the myriad other book apps available within the App Store. In this tutorial we'll take a look at the former method, and explain how easy it is to copy eBooks from your computer to the iPad.

iTunes Sync eBooks to your iPad

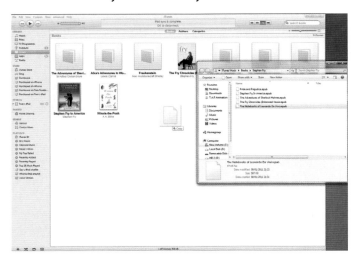

01 Drag and drop
Simply drag an ePUB or PDF file from your computer's desktop to the main window of iTunes. A Books tab will automatically be created in the Library.

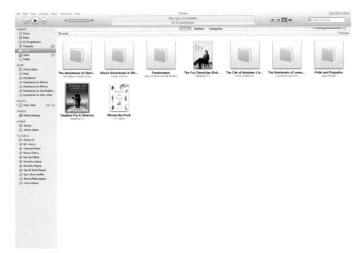

02 Books window
Turn on your iPad and plug it into the computer. After syncing, click on your iPad from the grey side bar, then the Books option at the top of the screen.

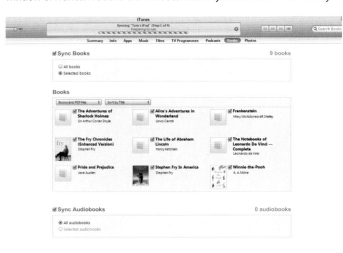

03 Choose your books
You can sync every book by checking the All Books button, or alternatively select your books of choice. Click the Sync/Apply button once you're ready.

04 iBooks
You can also download books from the iBooks app, found on the home screen of your device. For more information go to page 96.

Sync photos on your iPad

Discover how easy it is to sync photographs from your Mac/PC to an iPad

The iPad is the perfect device for displaying photos. Thanks to its Multi-Touch support it's easy to swipe through images, zoom into areas and create slide-shows. It's by far the best way to show off your latest holiday snaps as the device can be passed from person to person, and because the Photos app is so intuitive it can be used by anyone – even children.

There are a handful of ways to get your favourite photos onto your iPad. They can be synced from a Mac/PC, emailed or imported from an SD card. In this tutorial we'll explain how easy it is to transfer batches of images from your computer using iTunes. It only takes a few clicks, and because iTunes re-syncs images every time you plug the iPad into your Mac/PC you'll never have to manually transfer photos again.

iTunes Get your photos on your iPad

01 Plug in
Open iTunes on your Mac/PC, then plug the iPad into the computer and they'll sync. Once done, click on your iPad from the grey side bar on the left.

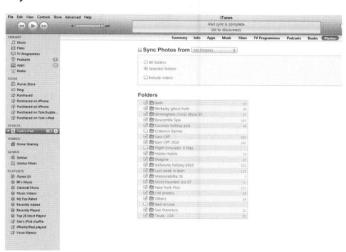

02 iPad summary
You'll see a summary of your iPad. At the top of the screen are various buttons for syncing media – click on the Photos button at the far end.

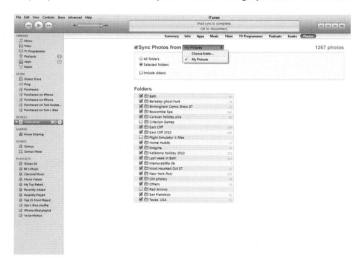

03 Choose your photos
Here you'll see an option to sync photos from your Mac or PC. Click on the check box and choose a folder from your computer. When correct, click OK.

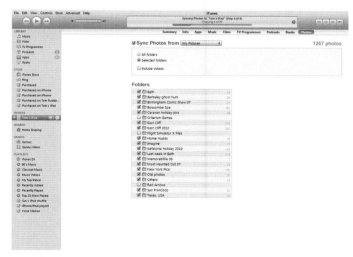

04 Get syncing
If sub-folders are present you can choose which to sync from the window below. Once you're happy, click the Apply button in the bottom-right corner.

Setting up

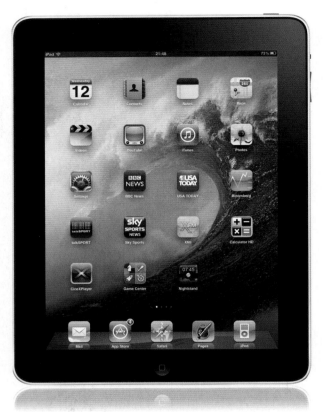

How to use iPad Settings

The Settings app is the epicentre of your iPad. Here you can customise everything from how apps work to the look and feel of the display

On the first page of the iPad screen is an app called **Settings**. This controls how your iPad works, allows individual apps to be configured and sets the look and feel of the screens. With it, you can enforce security, log on to Wi-Fi networks, save battery power, add signatures to emails, configure the web browser Safari to use specific search engines and much, much more. It is, perhaps, the most important app on your iPad. Learn what it has to offer and how you can change or configure things and you will take control of the iPad to make it work the way you want it to.

In this tutorial we are going to introduce you to some of the key features within Settings – the ones that you may want to check out straight away to get yourself acquainted to the system. More specific tutorials will follow to show you functions in more depth, but for now, let's delve into the nerve centre of this incredible piece of kit.

"Learn what the Settings have to offer and make the iPad work the way you want it to"

Settings Work your way around the iPad's control system

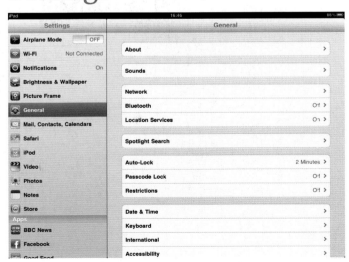

01 Into the Settings

Turn your iPad on and slide the bar across to unlock it. On the very first screen is the Settings app. Tap once on it to launch. There are a great number of parameters but you'll find a lot of useful things to tweak in the 'General' section. If this isn't automatically selected, tap on it now.

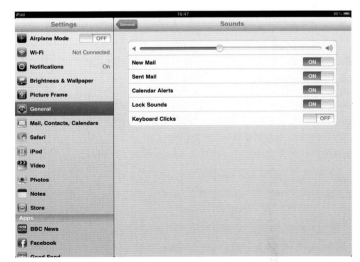

02 Changing the sounds

One of the first things to check out is the sound settings; tap on Sounds and customise these options by sliding the setting to On or Off and sliding your finger along the volume to change it. The General section also lets you control Bluetooth, Date & Time settings and much more so explore here.

The Settings menu laid out in full

Work your way around this user-friendly settings menu

Come fly with me

You can set your iPad to Airplane Mode to disable any wireless activity and make sure there isn't any interference with the plane's equipment or electronic devices

Knowledge base
Master the options

The Settings app controls lots of different features of the iPad and they are all available simply by tapping on the entry for each one and then making the changes required. Some of the most useful include using a graphic equaliser with your music, different fonts with Notes and selecting from Google, Yahoo! Or Bing as your search engine in Safari. To set the music preference, tap on the iPod entry and then on EQ and you can select from a range of music styles and also boost or reduce the base and optimise for speech.

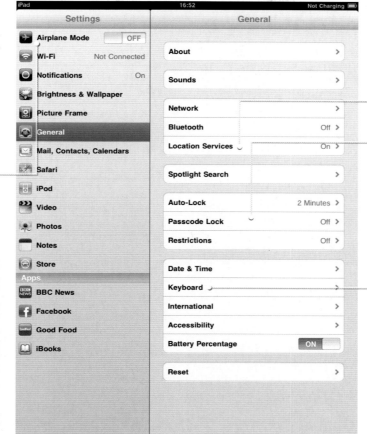

Location, Location

Tap on this section to turn on or off the location services. This allows the iPad to find your co-ordinates using GPS, Wi-Fi and cellular data for things like the Map app

Lock settings

Use Auto-Lock to decide how long you want the iPad to wait for inactivity before it locks, and use Passcode Lock if you want to set a password for when you turn on your iPad

Keyboard control

Here you can turn on or off the following functions: Auto-Capitalization, Auto-Correction, Check Spelling, Enable Caps Lock and the shortcut for full stops

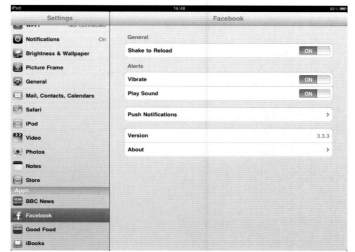

03 Enable Restrictions

The General section also has one of the most important settings options, especially if you let your kids play with the iPad. Here you can turn off in-app purchases, access to iTunes and much more. Just tap Enable Restrictions and you are prompted to set a passcode. Make it memorable.

04 App Settings

The Settings menu also lets you change the options for any apps you have downloaded. Just tap on the app you want to change the settings on and you have access to the options. As usual, move sliders to On or Off depending on your preferences to that function.

How to set up Wi-Fi

There are a host of services on the iPad, but you'll need to get online. We show you how to do just that

For all the iPad's uses and versatility, it doesn't really come into its own until you have Wi-Fi access. Sure you can play games, write documents, send emails and even download the latest books, but you can't do anything of it if you don't have access to the internet.

Internet access turns your iPad from an impressive piece of expensive kit into something that opens up worlds. This in part is due to the magnificence that is the App Store, a virtual store that gives you access to literally thousands of different applications, ranging from popular games like *Angry Birds* and *Real Racing* to GPS devices, interactive encyclopedias, word processing apps and much, much more.

Your iPad is a portal to a host of fantastic services, but first you need to give it access to the internet – then your options become plentiful. Follow our simple instructions in this easy-to-follow tutorial and unleash the potential of Apple's powerful device. You won't regret it.

Settings Switch on Wi-Fi on your iPad

01 Getting started
Go to the very first page of your iPad and look for the icon featuring one large cog and two small ones. Once found tap it once to enter your settings.

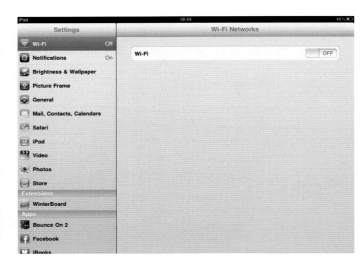

02 Locate Wi-Fi
After entering Settings look to the left-hand side. The first option is Wi-Fi. Tap on it and then turn Wi-Fi on by sliding the button.

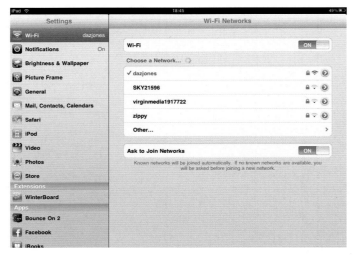

03 Find your connection
Your iPad will now start looking for available connection points. Ignore Ask to Join Networks at the bottom and simply tap on your connection.

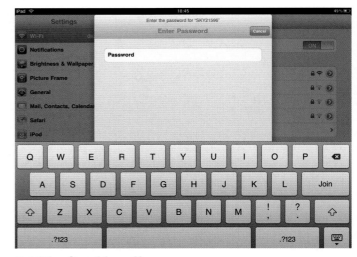

04 The final hurdle
You are now ready to enter your personal code. Fill in your details using the keyboard. Once filled in select Join on the virtual keyboard and you're done.

How to set up 3G

Access the internet while away from your home

3G is a network service that allows you to access the internet while away from a Wi-Fi signal. It's an amazingly useful service, due to the fact that as communication networks expand, online access is becoming more expensive. While Wi-Fi spots are becoming more numerous (everywhere from pubs to McDonalds has them) there can still be charges.

Luckily this is where 3G comes in. Frustratingly, unlike the iPhone, there is a charge for 3G usage on an iPad. Fortunately, it's not too unreasonable and the benefits of never being without an internet connection do make it worth the initial outlay. You do, however, need a 3G iPad, as some models are Wi-Fi only, but if you have the right hardware, we show you how to turn 3G on.

Settings Turn on 3G on your iPad

01 Find your settings

Enter your Sim on the side of your iPad then go to Settings – it's the icon that features a large cog and two smaller ones on the first page. Tap on it.

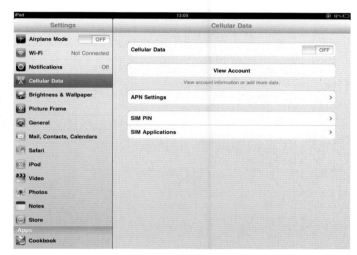

02 Accessing your cell

In Settings, select Cellular Data on the left-hand side and switch Cellular Data on (slide your finger across it). Now tap on View Account.

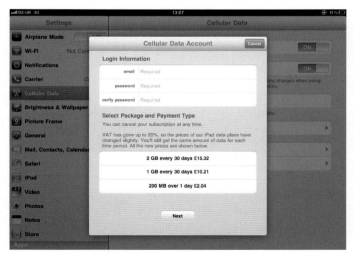

03 Decision time

You will be guided through questions. Fill in your details and decide which of the 3G services you wish to use. Press enter and you're all ready to go.

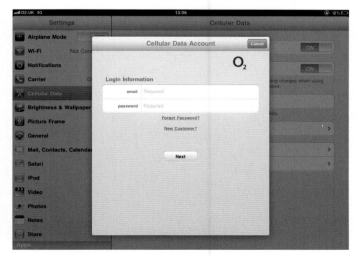

04 Don't forget

Should you wish to make changes, click the View Account tab from step 2. You'll be asked to put in your email and password to re-access your account.

How to access email on your iPad

While email works perfectly well on the iPhone it really comes into its own on the iPad's larger screen. This handy tutorial will let you set up your own personal account

In today's digital age using email is one of the most essential ways of being able to stay in touch with friends and family, as well as being a pretty vital tool in the business world. While both the iPhone and iPod touch are perfectly capable of displaying email, the iPad is just so much better due to its larger size, making it a much superior option. The virtual keyboard makes it far easier and quicker to type on (especially when you need to write longer mails) making it far more practical to use.

This step-by-step tutorial will not only show you how to set up a new or existing email account for use on the iPad and beyond, but will also take you through the fundamentals of reading and sending email. Once set up you'll be able to use existing accounts at will, quickly reply and forward mail that you receive, and, most importantly, ensure that you stay in touch with friends and loved ones. Basically you will never look at your iPad in the same way again.

"You will never look at your iPad in the same way again"

Settings Set up an email account on your iPad

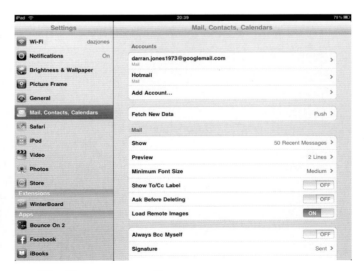

01 Setting things up

In order to set up an email account you will need to first enter the Settings of your iPad. Look at the icons on the first page of your iPad until you find one with a large cog and two smaller cogs. Tap on it to continue to the Settings menu.

02 Finding your mail

Upon entering Settings you'll find a row of different icons down the left-hand side of the screen. Look for and select 'Mail, Contacts, Calendars' in order to continue. Now look on the right-hand side of the screen and tap on Add Account…

Viewing mail

Look for the mail tab on the left-hand side of the page in Mail. Tap on it and you will instantly be shown your latest mail. Scroll down for more emails

Move items
Want to organise your mail? Simply tap the folder icon located at the top of the screen. You can then send your mail to a variety of different folders

Forwarding Mail
If you need to reply to an email hit the arrow icon near the top of the screen. You can then reply to the sender or forward the message on

Send email
Tap the tab in the top right-hand corner of your iPad to send mail. Fill out the address, add a subject and write your mail. Hit send when you're finished.

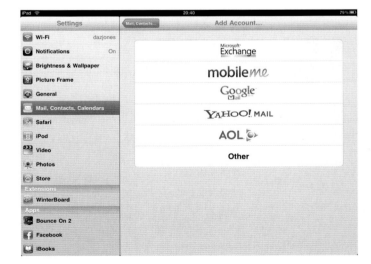

03 Make your choice
You'll now be presented with six different account options. They are Microsoft Exchange, MobileMe, Google Mail, Yahoo! Mail, AOL and Other (which will allow you access accounts like Hotmail). Whether you want to create a new account or add an existing one the process is as follows…

04 You've got mail!
After choosing your account you'll be presented with the following screen. All you need to do here is fill in the relevant information for each section. Once this is done simply tap on Save in the top right-hand corner. Congratulations, you have mail.

Setting up

Change Wallpaper on your iPad

We show you how to quickly customise the background of your home and lock screens

With the iPad, Apple has allowed users the ability to change the background of the home screen as well as the lock screen. This may seem like a trivial addition to the software set but for Apple it's pretty big. It is a company that deals in absolutes and who employs a closed system to prevent people making the environment look bad. So we're glad that we get to add a little individuality to the home screen and we're also pretty pleased when we discovered you can also have two different images for the lock screen and home screen.

Making changes to the system is very simple; it works in a very similar way to the iPhone, only you can see much more of the action path that you take to get to a change in settings. This makes the system clearer, more memorable and much easier to use. Proficiency at this simple task should give you the courage to explore the settings further to get even more use from your iPad and make improvements to the way it works for you. Whether it's an image from the iPad's supplied Wallpaper set or a photo from your album, following this step-by-step tutorial will instantly customise your iPad and have it looking the way you want it to.

Settings Change wallpaper

01 Cog tapper

Load the Settings by tapping the Settings button in the iPad home screen. You will be taken to this screen. Tap on Brightness & Wallpaper on the left-hand side.

02 Wallpaper

Here you can adjust the brightness if you deem it necessary. Simply tap on the pictures beneath the word 'Wallpaper' in the right-hand column of the screen.

03 Options

You now have several options from which to get a picture from. Choose the album that you wish to pick from. Tap on that album to then bring up the contents.

Customising your home screen

Making the most of all that screen real estate

Kill it
Apple also makes it easy for you to change your mind and go back to the last action. In this case just hit the Cancel button

Simplicity
As always Apple makes interfaces easy to use. There's no mass of dialogue and the system breeds confidence to try more complex tasks and procedures

Great resolution
The iPad screen has a fantastic 1024-by-768-pixel resolution at 132 pixels per inch (ppi) resolution for viewing images so having a cool pic behind your icons is a must

Finger fun
While positioning your picture you'll be able to see just how responsive the iPad touch screen is. It's a testament to hardware and software unity

Knowledge base

Settings
The settings system on the iPad follows the same pathways as those on the iPhone, only instead of shunting the view to the left or right as options are chosen, you can see the result of your choice to the right of the static options list.

04 Preview
Once in the album of your choice, make your final selection and then simply tap on that picture. A zooming animation will automatically take you to a preview screen.

05 Top options
Use a pinch, reverse pinch and swipe to position the image and then pick from the options at the top of the screen: you can pick Set Lock Screen, Set Home Screen or Set Both.

06 Check it
Once you've tapped an option you'll be taken back to the home screen where you can see your changes. Use the sleep button if you wish to view the lock screen.

Getting starte

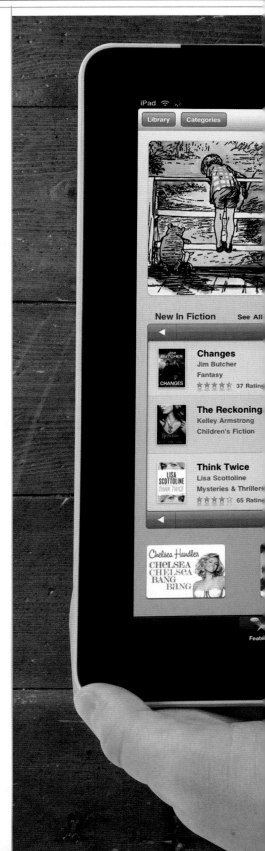

All the basics are covered right here to get you in control of your iPad

44 Moving icons and using folders
Keep your iPad organised

46 Work with multiple pages in Safari
Multitask your internet browsing

48 Get the most from bookmarks on the iPad
Save your favourite places in Safari

50 Change the default search engine
Use Yahoo! or Bing in the search bar

52 Organising emails
Set up, search, and use mailboxes

54 How to work with attachments
Learn how to work with email attachments

56 Set the default calendar
Change the default calendar to suit you

58 Add an Event in Calendar
Never miss an appointment again

60 Add a contact
Input people's details manually to your iPad

62 Creating, sending and receiving contacts
Learn how to sync, send and receive contacts

64 Use the iPad's Notes app
Find your way around this useful program

66 Save a Bookmark in Maps
Save your favourite places with ease

68 Get directions using Maps
Calculate routes and view directions

70 Send and receive locations with Maps
Let people know where you are quickly

72 Access video content via the YouTube app
Watch a world of videos on your iPad

74 Use the camera connection kit
Transfer photos to your device

76 Create a slideshow on the iPad
Show your pictures off in style

78 Set up a photo frame using your iPad
Turn your hardware into a digital photo frame

80 Get the most out of iPad videos
Watch mobile movies with ease

82 Easily create a song playlist using the iPod app
Get to know your iPad's iPod

84 Use iTunes on the iPad
Find your way around the iPad's iTunes

86 Use iTunes to get music
Fill your iPad with tunes

88 Use iTunes to get movies
Download films to your iPad

90 Use iTunes to get TV programmes
Learn how to download films to your iPad

92 Create and save Genius playlists on your iPad
Let your iPad make music selections for you

94 Use the App Store on your iPad
Search for and buy apps for your device

96 Download iBooks from the App Store
Open up a world of digital books

98 Purchase an iBook
Download an eBook and get reading

100 Getting to know iBooks
Work your way around this book app

102 Creating Bookmarks in iBooks
Never lose your place again

d

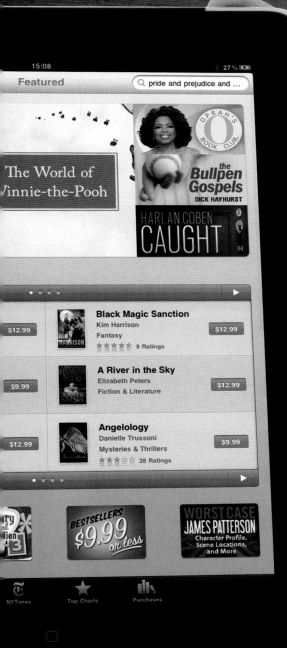

Tip one
Move icons

Tip two
Organise emails

Tip three
Access video content

Tip four
Use iTunes

"iBooks is magnificent in its simplicity, making impulse buys a regular occurrence"

Moving icons and using folders

Once you've installed lots of apps, the screens start to fill up and it gets harder to find things. Discover how to organise your apps and keep your iPad tidy

Whenever a new app is installed, it just gets added to the end of the existing list, or if there's a gap anywhere, it can appear there. This is fine when you only have a handful of apps, but after a couple of months with your iPad, the screens start to fill up and it all looks disorganised and messy. Fortunately it can all be organised into areas of similar functions, such as games on one page, utilities on another and reference apps on a page as well. You can reorganise your iPad screens using iTunes, where it is easy to create extra screens, even if the current ones are full, but it's also possible to move icons around directly on the iPad. Also, you can create as many folders as you like and bundle apps together to make your display very neat and tidy. Final benefits are that unwanted apps can be deleted and must-have apps can be added to the favourites bar at the bottom of every screen.

> "You can create as many folders as you like and bundle apps together to make your display tidy"

iPad Home Keep your iPad organised

01 Activate the wiggle
Turn your iPad on so that you are looking at your Home screen. If you have lots of apps then the icons for them will be spread over subsequent screens. To arrange them together tap and hold an app you want to move until all the apps start to wiggle.

02 Move the app
Still holding down on the app, drag your finger to the edge of the screen you want to move to. The apps will scroll sideways to give you the next screen. Move your finger over the place you want the app to go and then let go of it.

Inside the new folder display

How to edit the folder name and move and delete apps inside it

Edit the folder name
Tap a folder to open it. Tap and hold an app inside to go into wiggle editing mode. You can now remove or change the folder name

Take an app out
While in wiggle mode you can drag an app out of the folder again simply by tapping and holding and then moving outside the folder area

Rearrange apps inside the folder
If there's lots of apps inside a folder, rearrange them by tapping and holding and then dragging to a new position. The other apps will shuffle along and move

Delete an app in a folder
To remove an app that is inside a folder simply tap on the X gadget on the top-left corner. You will still have a backup inside iTunes

Knowledge base
Favourite and unwanted apps
When in wiggle mode a little cross appears on the top-left corner of all the apps. Tap on this to delete the app directly from your iPad. You can't delete the ones the iPad comes with. The favourites bar at the bottom of the screen comes with six slots for your favourite apps. Again, in wiggle mode you can move them around, drag them on or off the bar or simply add your new, favourite app to the ones there by dragging and releasing the app over it.

03 Create folders for common apps
Press the Home button to exit wiggle mode. To create folders though, drop an app over the top of one you want it to appear in a folder with. A folder is then instantly created with a name that reflects the type of apps if they are fairly similar.

04 Rename the folder
If the folder name isn't to your liking, simply tap on the X gadget to delete it and tap in the text field to enter your own. When complete, press the Home button twice to exit. To add more apps to the same folder, simply drag and drop them into it.

Work with multiple pages in Safari

Browsing the web on the iPad is completely different to doing so on your Mac or PC. It's obviously similar to the iPhone with a few subtle differences…

When Apple revealed the iPhone back in January 2007, it introduced the general public to the notion of holding the internet in your hands and manipulating it with your fingers. In one fell swoop, the idea of creating a simplified internet for mobile devices because they supposedly couldn't handle "proper" webpages was destroyed forever.

All the features you've been used to on your iPhone have been transferred over to the iPad, but the iPad isn't just a bigger version of its older sibling. The larger screen size enabled Apple's engineers to offer you more options and more control over how you interact with your webpage.

In this tutorial, we'll introduce you to the basics of Safari and having multiple windows open at the same time. The principle is the same as on your iPod touch, but the implementation is quite different with the addition of new menus and the repositioning of existing buttons. So grab your iPad and let's get started.

"The larger screen offers you more options and control over how you interact with your webpage"

Mobile Safari   Open multiple pages in Safari

01 Launch Safari
Tap on the Safari icon to open it and launch a webpage. You'll notice that contrary to the iPhone, all the navigation controls are at the top sharing space with the address bar and Google search field.

02 Multiple thumbnails
Tap on the multiple-page icon, third from the left on the toolbar, to reveal a new part of the interface. If this is the first time you've done this, you'll notice a smaller thumbnail of your existing page and another called 'New Page'.

Web navigation
Getting to know the functions

Bookmark bar
This Bookmark bar is only revealed when either the address field or Google search field is selected and the keyboard is up. Hide the keyboard and the bar disappears as well

Save an address
Use this button if you want to save the page you're currently reading into your Bookmark section. You can also use it to email the link as well

Bookmark list
To see all your bookmarks, tap on this button. You can also tap on that menu's Edit button to reorder them, create new folders, delete them, and so on

Open a new page
Tap and hold on a link to reveal a new popover menu from which you can choose to open that link as a new page, preserving the existing one

Knowledge base
Import Bookmarks from your Mac
There are two ways to make sure all the bookmarks you've accumulated on your Mac can be transferred to your iPad. One of these is through MobileMe: make sure you've ticked 'Bookmarks' in the System Preferences MobileMe Sync tab. If you don't have a MobileMe account, you can do this via iTunes once your iPad is connected to it.

03 A new page
Tap on that 'New Page' thumbnail to open it up. By default, the Google search field is pre-selected and your Bookmark bar is also displayed. Perform a search, access one of your bookmarks or type in the new address yourself.

04 Limited numbers
There's a limit to the amount of pages you can have open at any one time: nine. Once you've hit that number, you'll have to start deleting existing ones if you need to open others by tapping on the 'x', top left of a thumbnail.

Getting the most from bookmarks on the iPad

The iPad has many uses, but one of its main strengths is browsing the web.
Like the Mac the iPad uses Safari – here's how to get the most out of it

The iPad is great for many things and the extra applications available for it expand its usability even further. Some of the built-in applications will get more use than anything you download from the App Store, however. One of the apps you're likely to use more often than any other is Safari.

Though there are fewer features on the iPad version of Safari there's still a lot you can do with the application. Holding the internet in your hands is great and

really changes the way you browse and interact with the web. Though Safari shares its name with the Mac and PC equivalents, it's not exactly the same as those applications. The iPad version of Safari has been tweaked to work much better with the touch interface. Those of you with MobileMe accounts can also sync their bookmarks over the air with the iPad and Safari on your computer. You can also add sites to your home screen for easier access. Here we'll show you how to maximise Safari's bookmark potential.

Using bookmarks
Working your way
around Safari bookmarks

Bookmarks bar
You can store all your most oft-visited websites here but remember to turn the 'Show bookmarks' option on in Settings. If you edit the names you can store more links here too

Knowledge base
MobileMe
If you have a MobileMe account you can sync your bookmarks from your computer to your iPad, that way you won't have to add them all manually. To make sure you are syncing your bookmarks go to Settings and Mail, Contact, Calendars. Tap on your MobileMe email address and then make sure that Bookmarks is set to On.

Add bookmark icon
The most useful icons are here. Add a new page, see your bookmarks and when you want to add a bookmark, tap here to start the process off

Address bar
Of course, you can still just get to your favourite website the old fashioned way by typing them directly into the address bar

Search
The search bar is visible all the time and by default is set to Google, but if you want you can switch from Google to Yahoo! if you prefer

Safari for iPad   Get to grips with bookmarks in Safari on the iPad

01 Add a website
Navigate to the website you want to add to your home screen. When it has loaded tap on the + symbol in the toolbar and tap Add to Home Screen.

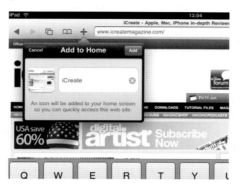

02 Give your icon a name
When you tap on Add to Home Screen it will add the title of the page, but you can edit this to something more appropriate. Tap Add when you're done.

03 Get rid of a home screen icon
If you're not using your bookmarked home screen icon very much, it's easy to get rid of it. Tap and hold until the x appears at the top right and tap that.

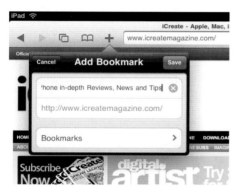

04 Add a bookmark
You'll be familiar with internet bookmarks and you can add them on the iPad too. Tap the + symbol on the toolbar and then Add bookmark.

05 Name your bookmark
After you've tapped on Add bookmark you'll have to give your new bookmark a name. This will be automatically chosen, but you can easily change it.

06 Get to your bookmarks
To see your bookmarks tap on the icon next to the + symbol in the toolbar. Your bookmarks will be listed under the History and Bookmarks Bar folders.

07 Delete a bookmark
To remove a bookmark from your folder tap on the bookmarks icon and then tap on Edit. A red icon with a – symbol will appear; tap it and then tap Delete.

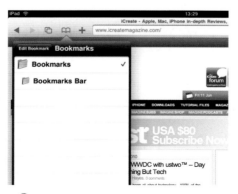

08 Move the bookmark
If you'd like to keep the bookmark in the bookmarks bar, tap Edit and then tap on your bookmark. Available folders will appear, so tap the Bookmarks Bar folder.

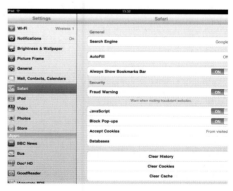

09 Show the Bookmarks bar
The bookmarks bar may not be showing up for you; it's easy to remedy this. Go to Settings>Safari and make sure that Always Show Bookmarks Bar is set to on.

Change the default search engine

The built-in search bar in Safari lets you seek out what you need fast, but you don't have to just use Google to provide your answers, Yahoo! is an option too

When you're searching the web it's probably second nature to just tap on the toolbar and type out your enquiry. By default Apple has chosen to use Google as the search engine of choice and for many people this will be absolutely fine.

However, Google isn't to everyone's tastes so there's the option to swap to Yahoo! or Bing. As it stands, if you use Safari for your web browsing these are your only choices and you can't even pick your favourite location. For instance, you can't set UK as the location for your preferred results. Some of the third-party web browsers available on the App Store will let you choose from a wider range of default search partners.

Otherwise you can, of course, navigate to the homepage of your favourite search engine and set it as an icon on your home screen. This way you'll always start a new browsing session at your desired search engine. However, for the built-in search bar in Safari you're stuck with just the three until Steve Jobs decides that more are needed.

"If Google isn't to your tastes so you can swap to Yahoo! or Bing"

Safari on iPad   Swap default search providers on your iPad

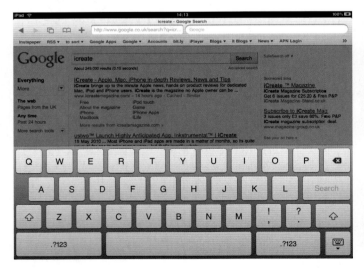

01 Safari search

If you open Safari you'll see the search bar up in the top-right of the screen. In it will be the name of the current default search engine provider, for example in the screenshot above it's Google. When you begin typing the name disappears.

02 Settings

You can't change the search provider within Safari; instead you have to do it from within the Settings app. You need to press the Home button to quit the app and navigate back to your home screen. Find the Settings app and then tap on it.

Search engine selection

Find the perfect search engine for you

Search bar

The search bar in Safari can use either Google, Yahoo! and Bing, you can swap between them but sadly you can't choose another provider if you prefer the competition

Add a Bookmark

You can add your own favourite search engine to the home screen by creating a bookmark. Tap on the + symbol and choose Add to Home Screen

Search

When you tap into the search bar the on-screen keyboard pops up automatically. Cleverly, the Return key is swapped for the search command so simply hit that to get the results you want

Suggested results

Both Yahoo! and Google offer suggestions based on what you type, that way you don't always have to type the search term fully. Simply tap on the suggestion to immediately see the associated results appear

Knowledge base

Third-party browsers

You don't have to use Safari on the iPad as there are a number of alternative browsers available on the App Store. These offer more in the way of functionality too, such as tabbed browsing and a larger range of search provider options. Simply type 'web browser' into the App Store search bar and download a selection; some are free, others available for a small fee.

03 Safari settings

In the Settings app you will see the list of options down the left-hand side of the screen. By tapping on Safari you will reveal the options that are available to you. In the main section on the right, tap on Search Engine up at the top, listed under General.

04 Make your selection

The scarcity of options here and size given over to show them off would seem to imply that more search engine options could be accommodated. As it stands, however, you have just the three to choose from. Tap on Google, Yahoo!, or Bing and return to Safari.

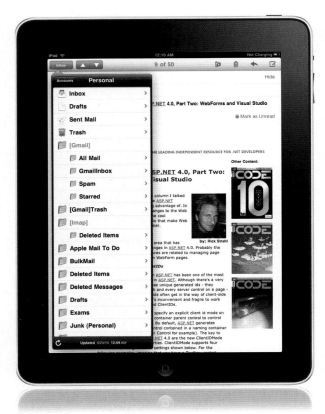

Organising emails

The Mail app on the iPad sets a new standard on how emails are managed from touch-enabled tablet devices. In this tutorial we show you how to manage your email

Email is part of everybody's day-to-day life. Most of us start our morning with it. Before, checking for emails would mean starting your fully fledged computer, but with the introduction of the iPhone this habit changed drastically. Most of us were using the device to check emails, but even though the iPhone has a decent Mail application, the small screen and lack of full-size keyboard was a problem. iPad's Mail app, however, takes what is good about it on the iPhone and presents it with large screen and full-size keyboard. This provides the best email experience between the mobile devices.

The Mail app supports most of the current generation technology such as automatic service discovery, Exchange Support, POP/IMAP support and built-in support for MobileMe, Gmail, Yahoo Mail and AOL. The Mail app on the iPad also plays well with other related apps on the iPad, such as the Calendar.

In this tutorial we will look into doing a few of the more important tasks using the Mail app. It's all very easy – let us show you how…

> **"The iPad takes what is good about Mail on the iPhone and presents it with a full-size keyboard"**

Mail Organising emails

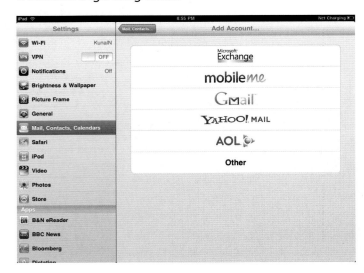

01 Adding an email account

Open Settings and select 'Mail, Contacts, Calendars'. You will now be presented with account types that you can use. Tapping on any one of the supported services will open the pop-up window asking for account details. Fill in the required information to set up your email account.

02 Searching for emails

Search for emails in Mail by typing onto the Search Box and selecting the From, To or Subject fields. Do a full text search by tapping All. By default this will only do a search on the emails that have been downloaded on the iPad. To do a full search you can tap on 'Continue Search on Server…'

You've got mail!

Working your way around the Mail app

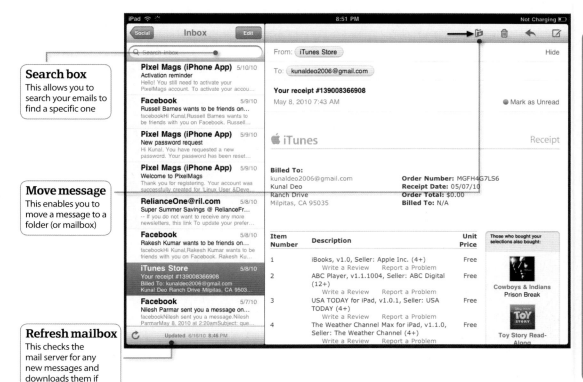

Search box
This allows you to search your emails to find a specific one

Move message
This enables you to move a message to a folder (or mailbox)

Refresh mailbox
This checks the mail server for any new messages and downloads them if they are available

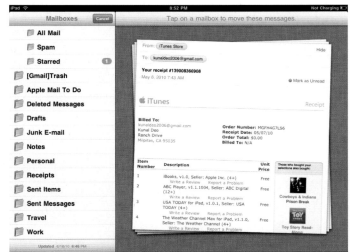

03 Moving messages between folders (mailboxes)

Tap Edit, then select all the messages that you want to move to a different folder, then tap Move. Tapping Move will give you a list of the folders that are available; all you need to do is simply tap on a folder to move the selected messages.

04 Tweak the settings

You can configure a wide range of settings which control how Mail works. To access the settings for Mail, tap Settings (from the home screen), then 'Mail, Contacts, Calendars'. You can change the Account Settings, Mail, Default Account, Signature and more.

How to work with attachments

The iPad is better suited for work than an iPhone, and it's especially useful for emailing documents while on the move. We'll show you how the iPad deals with attachments

It's hard to imagine a working day when you don't have to deal with email attachments, and it's likely you're going to be faced with similar tasks while on your iPad. So, how does the iPad handle these? That question will depend on what's attached to your email in the first place.

This step-by-step tutorial will show you how you can work with your iPad to handle common files like photos, iWork or Microsoft Office documents and

PDFs. They each behave in slightly different ways but the principle is actually very similar and it will take you next to no time to find your way around the iPad interface.

But receiving attachments is only half the story. It's obvious that you'll also need to send them out too, which is why we'll cover that part as well. So pick up your iPad and let's see how all of this works.

Email analysis

We break down the iPad's email and let you know all of the key functions and associated icons

Knowledge base

Send more than one photo attachment

To send multiple photos in the same email message, you need to start from your Photo app's thumbnail section. Tap on the Export button (top right of the interface) and select up to five photos – that's the limit. Although you can copy more and manually paste them to an email, this may fill up the recipient's mailbox, which they might not be too happy about.

The paper clip

Any email containing an attachment will have this little paper clip next to the sender's name. Most of the time, the file will appear as an icon at the bottom of the message

Specialised icons

If the file can be opened in one of your iPad's apps, it'll bear that app's image at the centre of its icon. If the icon is bare it'll only be viewable with Quick Look

Editing attachments

To open a file in another program, tap and hold on the file's icon to reveal this popover menu. A simple tap on the right option will transfer it to that program

Downloading attachments

If you see this downward-pointing arrow on an attachment, it means it hasn't been downloaded to your iPad yet. To get it, tap on it

Mail Send and receive email attachments

01 Into the Photo app

When you're sent an image, adding it to your photo library is easy: tap and hold on it to reveal a popover menu. Select Save Image.

02 RTF and PDF files

If you're dealing with RTF files or PDFs, tapping on its icon will open it in Quick Look, where you can view and copy text, but you can't edit anything.

03 iWork and Office documents

With other documents like Word or Pages, tapping on it will lead to the same Quick Look section, but if you need to edit it, there's another way.

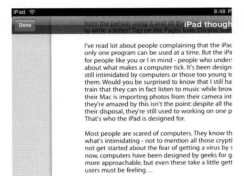

04 Getting out of Quick Look

To get out of Quick Look tap on the screen. You can choose Done to get back to Mail or Open in Pages if you own the Pages application. Do the former.

05 Open in an editing app

To get straight to Pages without going into Quick Look, tap and hold on the file's icon. This reveals a popover menu. Select Open in "Pages".

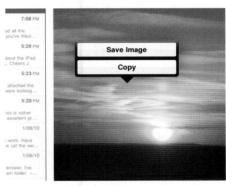

06 Copying a photo

Going back to a photo attachment, if you want to use it in iWork but not add it to your library, tap and hold on it, and select Copy from the popover menu.

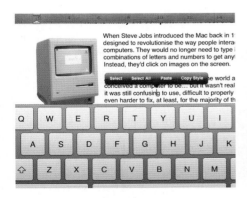

07 Pasting elsewhere

To open a document in Pages for instance (either an existing one or from an attachment), tap and hold to reveal a menu and select Paste to add that photo.

08 Attaching a file

To attach a file from one of your iWork apps, select a document from the Gallery, tap on the first button in the toolbar (lower left) and choose Send via Mail.

09 Attaching a photo

To send a photo, select it and tap on the same button, just as you did in the previous step. Only this time, it's located top right of the interface.

Set the default calendar

The iPad can handle multiple calendars so you can keep your work, home or family events separate, but you may use one more than another. Here we show you how to set the default

One of the main advantages of the iPad is its ability to manage multiple calendars in one very simple interface. You can mix and match your home and work commitments and keep them all in the same place. The colour-coded calendars mean you can know instantly whether the next date in your diary is home, work, or anything else related.

When you're making entries to Calendar on your iPad it selects a default calendar to store the event in. This is great if the default calendar matches the one you use most. However, if you're using it for mainly work-related stuff and the default calendar is for home, you'll have to change it each time you add an event. You can edit the entries to match the calendar after, but this is a time-consuming process.

Changing the default calendar will make entering new appointments that bit faster and cut down on mislabelled entries too. Of course, the time saved is minimal, but it's one less thing to worry about and will help to keep you more organised in the long run.

Calendar Change the default calendar

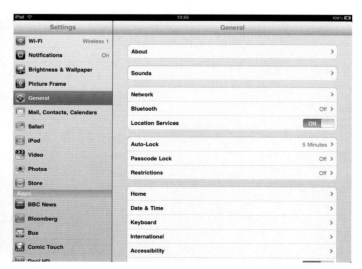

01 Go to Settings

A few of the iPad's application settings are editable from within the app itself, but in this case you need to go to Settings. Press the Home button and then swipe to the home screen with the Settings app on it. Simply tap it to open.

02 Mail, Contacts, Calendars

Over on the right-hand side of the Settings screen you will see all the options available to you and in most cases the General page will be showing. Tap on Mail, Contacts, Calendars just below General to get to the Default Calendar.

Defining the default calendar
Keeping you in the right place at the right time

Default calendar
Each new entry will be put in the default calendar. You can change the default by following the steps here or for one-offs simply tap on Calendar

Calendars
If you have a number of calendars, you can choose which ones to display by tapping on Calendars at the top-left of the screen. When the list appears simply tap on the tick to hide those entries

Add event
Add a new event by tapping on the + symbol in the bottom right-hand corner of Calendar on your iPad. To edit the settings simply tap on each heading

Knowledge base

Repeat event
If you want to set a regular reminder, for someone's birthday or perhaps a regular but finite set of meetings, then tap on repeat and select the appropriate frequency. You will notice that there's a new option in the Add Event pop-up called End Repeat. Tap here and you can choose the exact date you want the repeat to finish or leave it to repeat forever.

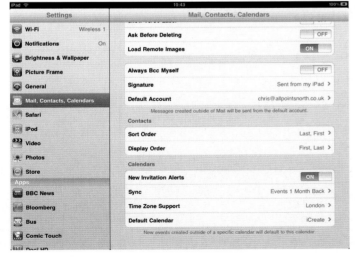

03 Default Calendar
You will need to scroll down by swiping to get to the Default Calendar setting as it is right at the bottom of the page. In the Calendars section the current default calendar will be showing; you can tap on it to access further options that are available.

04 Select your calendar
Here you have a list of all the calendars that are available to you and the currently selected default has a tick next to it. Simply tap on the calendar you would like to select as the new default. Press the Home key when you're done.

Add an Event in Calendar

Make sure you never miss an important event with your iPad

The Calendar app on the iPhone is pretty useful and very easy to use, but it gets absolutely dwarfed by the sheer scale and beauty of the iPad equivalent. Like the Contacts app, Apple has gone with the classic analogue look and made the app look like an old-school, physical calendar. Of course, this digital version has a multitude of advantages over a real one. Firstly, you get the beauty of typeface rather than scrawled handwriting; secondly, there's no need for Tipp-Ex; and thirdly, you can view it in a number of different ways. We could go on and on.

Like all the iPad apps, the Calendar app is easy to use. So easy to use that you'll want to document every move you make using it, from eating breakfast to scheduling toilet breaks. Adding an event is simplicity itself, and the large screen size means that pop-up windows replace the screen shunting right or left as it does on the iPhone. All you need remains in front of you at all times. Once your events are created they can be edited and you can view them in a number of ways as you change orientation or as you dictate on the top tabs of the app.

Adding an event

You're never more than a few taps away from adding or editing an event to your calendar, and the interface is extremely simple

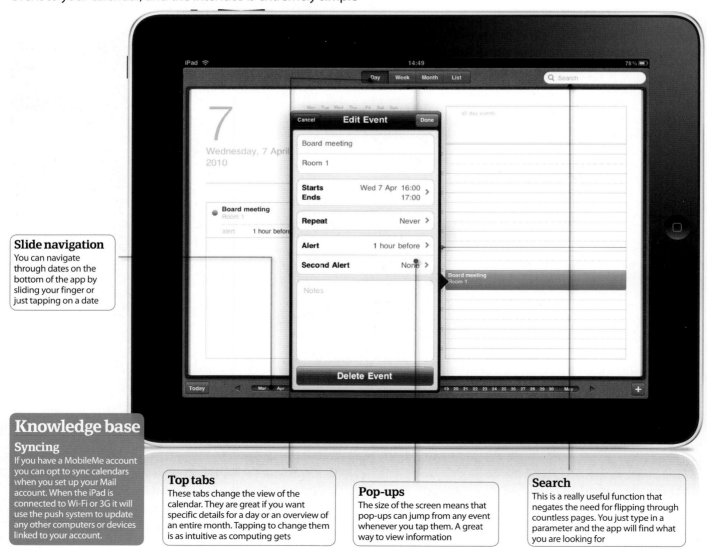

Slide navigation
You can navigate through dates on the bottom of the app by sliding your finger or just tapping on a date

Knowledge base

Syncing
If you have a MobileMe account you can opt to sync calendars when you set up your Mail account. When the iPad is connected to Wi-Fi or 3G it will use the push system to update any other computers or devices linked to your account.

Top tabs
These tabs change the view of the calendar. They are great if you want specific details for a day or an overview of an entire month. Tapping to change them is as intuitive as computing gets

Pop-ups
The size of the screen means that pop-ups can jump from any event whenever you tap them. A great way to view information

Search
This is a really useful function that negates the need for flipping through countless pages. You just type in a parameter and the app will find what you are looking for

Calendar Add an event

01 Open the app
Open the Calendar app and turn the iPad horizontal to see the dual-page layout. Navigate to the day you want and then tap the plus button on the bottom left.

02 Pop-up
An iPhone-sized pop-up window appears, as does the keyboard. Tap the field you wish to edit and then name your event.

03 Detail
You can add as much or as little detail as you want, including the location of the event. You have access to a full keyboard so you can go to town on the detail.

04 Time it
You now need to add the start and end date of your event. Tap on the relevant field to see the pop-up change into a new window display.

05 Familiar wheels
Use the wheels to select the times and dates that you want to use. You can also toggle the All-day button instead if you wish.

06 Done it
When you have everything in place, you need to tap the Done button. Alternatively you can cancel it to return without saving.

07 Alert
Tap the Alert field to set reminders for the event. These will pop up on your iPad at the times you set them. There are plenty of options.

08 Tap it, save it
Tap on the option you wish to use and a tick will appear. Save your progress by clicking the Done button on the top right.

09 Save and view
Save your event and then it will appear on the page. Tap on it to see the full details and to make changes or, if you want, delete the event.

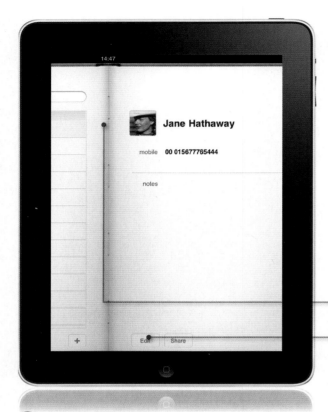

Add a contact
Update your contacts on the iPad

Now that you've finally got your hands on a shiny new iPad, one of the first things you're going to want to do is add a contact to the sumptuous Contacts app. It works in much the same way as the app on the iPhone; it still has easy-to-find buttons and an intuitive natural feel but rather than having the screen shunt to the right through each menu, you get very nice pop-up boxes that are easy to use and make even more sense than the iPhone ever did. If you're new to the whole touch concept then this process will be a revelation in simplicity. Not only can you add all the pertinent information you need but there are cool little extras that make the system very slick and easy to use.

The Contacts app will work in both landscape and horizontal mode but we found that having all that screen real estate was suited better, in this instance, to the horizontal mode. The app is designed to look like an actual physical book and it gives the whole process a nice old-world feel. You can literally feel your way around all of the apps on the iPad and the contacts app is no different. Remember that even if you make a mistake you can go back and edit anything you like over and over again. You can also sync existing contacts from iTunes into the app.

Edit
You can go back to any contact you want and edit their details by tapping on the Edit button at the very bottom of the page. It will take you back to the screen in step two

Detail
The book-like form and the attention to detail is incredible. You can even see the staples where the virtual book has been bound together

Contacts Add a people to your contacts

01 Open her up
Open the Contacts app from the home screen of your iPad and then use the '+' button, which can be found in the bottom right-hand side of the screen to begin adding the contact.

02 Tap and type
The keyboard will now appear and you can begin entering the necessary information. Tap on the field you wish to edit. A logical place to start is with the person's first name.

03 Cross it
As you type and get used to the keyboard you may make mistakes. You can use the backspace button to delete or remove everything using the little cross to the right of the field.

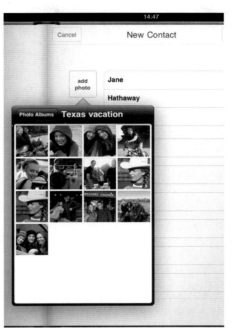

04 Add a photo

To add a photo just tap the add photo button and your photo albums (the ones you have synced) will magically appear. Tap on the one you wish to add from.

05 Take your pic

You can now choose from the pictures you have to hand. If there are more pictures than can fit in the pop-up window then you can scroll up and down in the window using a flick of the finger.

06 Move and scale

You now have to move and scale the picture you have selected. Those of you with an iPhone will be used to this. Use a pinch or reverse pinch to zoom in and out of the picture.

07 Use or cancel

Once the picture is how you would like it tap on the Use button on the top-right of the pop-up window. The picture you have selected will then slide into the photo area of the contact form.

08 Add fields

Go through the rest of the form and add as much or as little information as you need. Just tap into a field to edit it and the keyboard will spring up from the bottom of the screen.

09 Done

Once you are completely finished all you need to do is hit the Done button in the top-right of the page to save the changes and then simply return to the address book.

Getting started

Creating, sending and receiving contacts

Contacts on the iPad is a feature-rich contact management system. In this tutorial, we will show you how to create, send and receive contacts

As discussed on the previous page, contacts on the iPad are managed using a built-in app called Contacts. It provides easy access to all your contacts without needing a phone or a PC. It also allows you to store information for each contact, such as address, birthday, notes etc. But it is much more than just that, as Contacts is integrated with other apps, such as Maps and Mail. You can use the Maps app to show a contact's location, the same way you can also add an address to a contact.

Contacts allows you to sync with a variety of services, such as Google Contacts, Yahoo! Address Book, MobileMe, Microsoft Exchange Server and LDAP (Lightweight Directory Access Protocol) Server. Contacts makes it very easy to search for the contact information. If you have a Microsoft Exchange account on your iPad, you may also be able to search your enterprise Global Address List (GAL) for contacts in your organisation. But one of the most prominent features of Contacts is sharing. Sharing allows you send a contact in vCard (.vcf) format using email. Similarly, you can receive a shared contact as a vCard attachment in Mail. We will look into creating, syncing, sending and receiving contacts.

Contacts Learn your way around the Contacts app

01 Create a contact
As discussed on the previous page, it is very simple to add contacts. To recap: open Contacts, tap '+' to open the New Contact form and enter the details. You can tap 'Add new address' to add an address to the contact and tap 'Add field' to add additional fields. Tap Done to save the new contact.

02 Add contacts via syncing
You can also add contacts another way. Syncing Contacts allows you to access your contacts from other locations and services. To do this, you can use iTunes to sync Address Book contacts on your PC or Mac or use your iPad to add a Microsoft Exchange Server, MobileMe, or LDAP server.

Use the iPad's Contacts app

Search, share and edit your contacts

Edit contact
This button only works for the contact that is currently open. Make the changes and tap Done

Search in Contacts
Search for Contacts provides a way to search for contact details. You can search by using any contact field, such as First Name, Last Name or using the contact number

Share Contact
On the iPad, you can only use email to share a contact. Tapping Share will open a new email

Add contact
The '+' button lets you add a new contact. You can tap '+' to open the New Contact Form. Enter various details then tap Done to add a contact

Knowledge base

LDAP (Lightweight Directory Access Protocol)
LDAP is a client-server protocol for accessing a directory service. It was initially used as a front-end to X.500, but can also be used with standalone and other kinds of directory servers. LDAP lets you locate organisations, individuals, and other resources such as files and devices in a network, whether on the internet or on a corporate intranet.

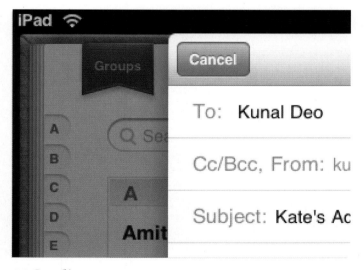

03 Sending a contact

To send a contact, open the contact you want to send then tap Share. A new Mail Compose window with the attached 'vcf' file will now open. Fill in the necessary details such as To, Subject and Body inside the Mail Compose window, then tap Send to send the contact.

04 Receive a contact

On the iPad you can receive a shared contact as a vCard (.vcf) attachment inside an email. Open the email with the contact and tap the '.vcf' file to open the contact details. Tap 'Create New Contact' or 'Add to Existing Contact' to save the information into an existing contact.

Use the iPad's Notes app

Don't feel you need to purchase Pages in order to jot down
ideas on your iPad – you can do this with Notes

Despite the fact that some people view the iPad as a device designed merely to consume media, just spending a few minutes with it will make you realise that this is complete nonsense. With the help of a few choice programs, the iPad is very capable of being used to create drawings, edit photos or even write essays. But you actually don't need to purchase anything for the latter, as the Notes app comes bundled with the iPad and is a really great place to start exploring how you can handle typing on glass. You may find it a lot easier than you think, and this built-in app can actually handle a variety of different tasks.

Notes is remarkably similar to the program bearing the same name on the iPhone and iPod touch, it has simply been expanded a little to take advantage of the additional space the iPad screen provides. This step-by-step tutorial will show you how it works, what you can do with it, and how it could help you in your day-to-day activities.

Notes app on iPad
The Notes app is great for jotting down ideas on the go,
and even copying text from the web to read later…

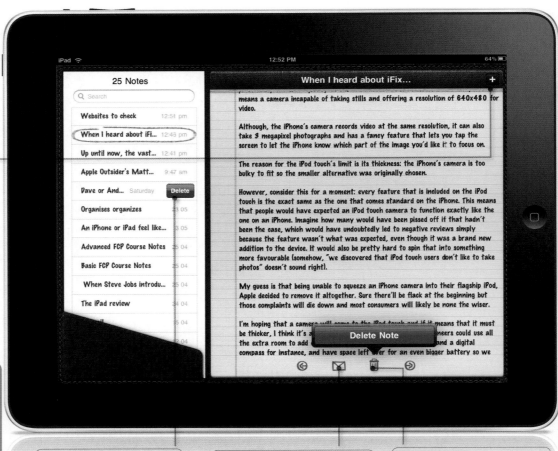

Add
You can add as many notes as you need. Whether you're in the landscape or portrait orientation, this button is always top-right of the screen

Swipe
You don't have to select a note to delete it, just swipe its title to reveal this Delete button – just like the messages in Mail

Emailing
Notes lets you email the content of your pages without you having to copy and paste the information yourself. Tap on this icon to create an email message

Delete
If you no longer need a particular note, select it and tap on this button. You'll be asked to confirm your choice just in case you tapped on it by mistake

Notes Use Notes to write down ideas

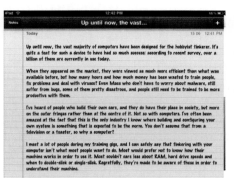

01 The look of Notes

Hold your iPad in the portrait orientation and tap the Notes app. Tap on the screen to reveal the keyboard. Now you can begin typing.

02 The '+' button

When you've finished, tap on the keyboard symbol with the down arrow (bottom-right of the keyboard) to dismiss it, then tap on the '+' button.

03 From one to another

That last action created a new note. You can swap between the first one and the one you're working on by tapping on the arrow buttons.

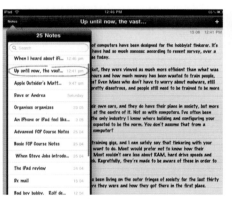

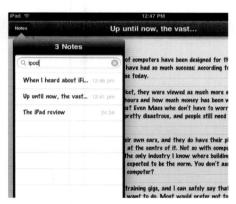

04 Pop-up menu

If you want to see all the pages you've created, tap on the Notes button to reveal a pop-up menu. They're presented in the order you created them.

05 The selected note

Whichever note is currently selected has a big red circle around its title. You can swipe down to reveal more notes, if you have them.

06 Searching

There's also a search field at the top of the pop-up menu, which can help you narrow down your search when you're looking for specific information.

07 Landscape

Turn the iPad to the landscape orientation. The notes don't get any wider, but your list becomes permanently available on the left-hand side.

08 Tappable links

If you type in a web link, it'll become active as soon as you hide the keyboard. Tap on it and you'll be sent to Safari. Tapping an email address sends you to Mail.

09 Save numbers

iPad also recognises phone numbers. Since you can't phone people, you're offered two other options: to Create New Contact or Add To Existing Contact.

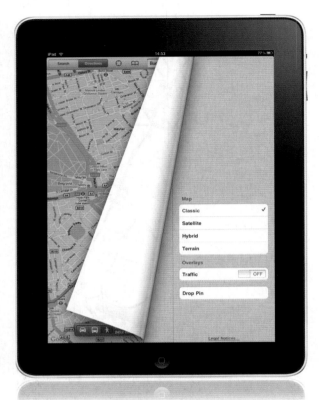

Save a bookmark in Maps

Save your favourite places easily in this app

It's a strange situation, really, because the Maps app is an incredibly useful addition on the iPhone and one that we've used countless times while we're out and about, but for some reason it hadn't really registered as a big deal on the iPad. That was until we loaded it and saw just how incredible it is on the huge iPad screen and how the Apple engineers have made the same technology so snappy and responsive. The way the maps render so much quicker is one of the clearest ways we've found to visually compare the processing power of the iPad versus the iPhone. Playing around with this app really is pure fun, but that shouldn't detract from the practical side that a huge map can have. With this in mind, it's useful to know how to quickly search for items and save them so that they can be called upon at any time. Like the iPhone version, this iPad Maps app is very simple to use and has some very cool detailing, which would have gone unnoticed on the smaller iPhone screen. The only drawback on the Wi-Fi-only iPad is that it's not a great portable app.

> "Playing around with this app is pure fun, but that shouldn't detract from the practical side"

Maps Adding a location bookmark

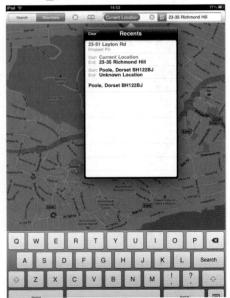

01 Load it, tap it

Load Maps from your home screen and begin your search by tapping your finger on the address/location field at the top of the interface. Type it in or search for your current location.

02 Type it, watch it

Once you've typed in your place and hit the search button, a pin will drop in the location. This should happen with satisfying speed. Above the pin the location should be named.

03 View change

You can change the view of the location in question by activating the hidden menu. To do this, use your finger to curl back the right-hand corner of the map. Tap on a view option.

Space everywhere

Like every other app on the iPad, Maps makes full use of the big screen by throwing pop-up windows of information into the middle of the screen

Cool clarity
The full zoom on the Maps app lets you see the planet in really stunning detail. The speed with which this app can do this only adds to the mesmerising nature of the experience

My location, different location
The 'My Location' button is situated at the top of the app window in the iPad version. Tap it to have your own location triangulated automatically

Toggle it
On the top left of the interface is the toggle switch between the search function and the directions function. Like the iPhone version, Maps on the iPad can act as a sat-nav system

Knowledge base
Super speed
The speed of the Maps app comes down to the Apple-made A4 processor and the RAM chip it's connected to working together to make a much snappier experience. The maps render much faster than the iPhone 3GS.

04 Zoom it
Use a pinch or reverse pinch to zoom in and out of the map so you can get an idea of what surrounds the location. You could be looking for nearby tube stations or bus stops, for example.

05 Closer look
You can also get in nice and close to your location and see exactly what it looks like. To begin adding it as a bookmark you need to hit the 'i' button next to the tag.

06 Roomy view
The info box will now spring up and you can use the button at the bottom to add the location to your Maps bookmarks. This process can be repeated for every location you want to add.

Get directions using Maps

One of the most prominent features of the Maps application is directions. You can get directions between any two locations or nearby places. Directions are intuitive and easy to follow on the iPad's giant screen

The Maps application on the iPad is more usable than it is on the smaller devices as there's a lot less scrolling involved. It is almost like using a paper map. Things like Traffic and Street View look brilliant on the larger screen, and Maps also has a new Terrain view that adds a layer of topographical data to the maps.

Maps on the iPad can be used to get directions between two places. It pulls out a lot of useful information related to a route that is very useful for a commuter, such as Driving/Transit/Walking Directions, Distance and Time to Commute. When using Transit Directions it also shows you the Transit Timings to help you plan ahead. You can also make use of the Traffic information when using directions, which will help you avoid unwanted delays. You can also use Google Street View to get a panoramic view of the destination, but note that this is not available on all the locations. The locations where it is available are indicated by the Street View icon.

In this tutorial we will find the directions from our office to McDonald's in Christchurch and satisfy our quench for tasty burgers, proving along the way just how well the Maps app works on the iPad.

Maps Get directions using Maps

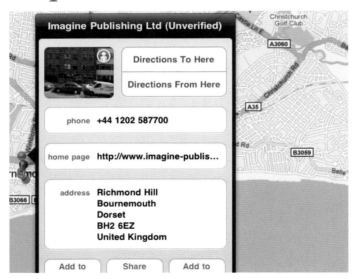

01 Set the Start Address

Search for a location on the map or, if you want to start from the current location, tap the My Location button in the bottom-left of the screen. Tap the pin to bring up the pop-up menu, and choose Directions From Here. Tap Directions, then enter the address. Now tap Search.

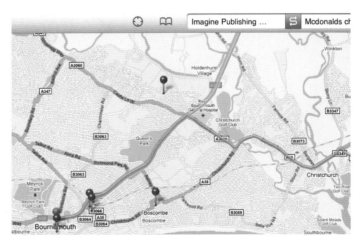

02 Set the destination address

Enter the destination location in the End box. In this case it is 'McDonald's, Christchurch'. In case there are multiple addresses for the searched address, Maps will put red pins for all the searched locations and set the destination to the one it finds most accurate. You can also select the address if it has already been searched previously. Now you can see the green pin connected by a blue line to a red pin. The green pin represents your start location, the blue line represents the route and the red pin represents the destination.

Get directions on your iPad
Use the Maps app to reach your destination

Current Location
Locate the current address with the help of any of the available GPS technologies

Reverse directions
Reverse the searched route

Start and destination locations
Green pins represent the start locations and red pins represent the destinations

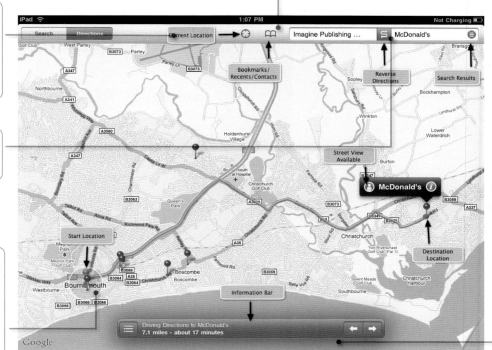

Knowledge base

GPS technology on iPad Wi-Fi and 3G

iPad Wi-Fi is an inferior GPS device when compared to iPad 3G. Wi-Fi depends on Skyhook Wireless Wi-Fi-based GPS technology to provide basic location specific data. Therefore it cannot be used where accurate GPS data is required. iPad 3G uses GSM and A-GPS in addition to Skyhook Wireless to determine location-specific information instead.

Views

To view your music collection in any of five different views simply tap on one of the five options. Making Genius mixes is simpler if you view your music as songs, however

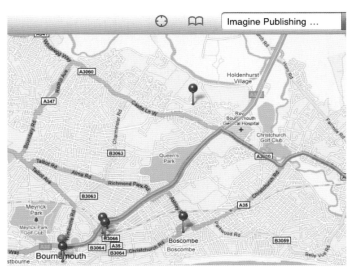

03 Getting the directions

Select the method of commute by tapping one of the icons in the top left-hand corner of the map. The options are for road, public transport or on foot. When a method is selected, the route map, the applicable distance and the expected time to reach your destination will be updated automatically.

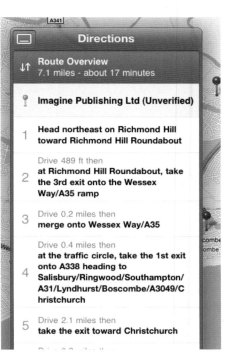

Directions

↕ **Route Overview**
7.1 miles - about 17 minutes

📍 **Imagine Publishing Ltd (Unverified)**

1   Head northeast on Richmond Hill toward Richmond Hill Roundabout

    Drive 489 ft then
2   at Richmond Hill Roundabout, take the 3rd exit onto the Wessex Way/A35 ramp

    Drive 0.2 miles then
3   merge onto Wessex Way/A35

    Drive 0.4 miles then
4   at the traffic circle, take the 1st exit onto A338 heading to Salisbury/Ringwood/Southampton/A31/Lyndhurst/Boscombe/A3049/Christchurch

    Drive 2.1 miles then
5   take the exit toward Christchurch

04 View turn-by- turn directions

Tap Start to view the turn-by-turn directions. Upon tapping Start you will get the driving directions on the blue bar. You can navigate through turn-by-turn directions using a swipe of a finger. Directions will indicate turns and distances so you can be sure you get the right one each time.

Getting started

Send and receive locations with Maps

Maps application on the iPad makes it very easy to share your location

The Maps application on the iOS platform is much more than just a map. It provides a wide range of things to do around maps, such as finding a route, studying geographical information, viewing real-time traffic information, viewing traffic, street views and much more besides. Among these there is a feature that is exceptionally useful called Share Location. To portray the usefulness of this little feature, let's say that while driving around you have discovered a cave that contains the treasure of Marco Polo. So you think you need to take it all now otherwise somebody else might discover it and take it. What will you do? You will open your iPad, find out the current location and then send an email with directions to the cave (using the Share Location feature), that's what.

In this step-by-step tutorial we will show you exactly how to share your location using the Maps app, so that you never miss an opportunity – especially one as big as this. Okay, so this kind of epic event won't happen to you all the time, but there are plenty of other occasions when rather than giving someone convoluted directions, you can just share your location easily using this method. It's really pretty easy, and here we show you how…

Maps Use the Maps app to let others know where you are

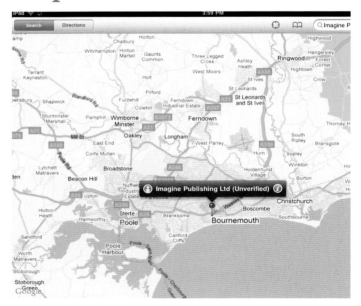

01 Locating the address

To begin, you need to locate the address you want to share. You can do this by searching your location in the search box or by dropping a pin on the location you want to share. A box will appear containing your location on screen.

02 Sharing the location

Once you have the correct location, tap on the pin to bring up the detailed information in a pop-up box. Tap the Share Location button available at the bottom of the window (you can also add the address to your contacts or bookmarks from here).

Use Maps to show friends where you are

Send your current location to friends via email

Simplicity
As always Apple makes interfaces easy to use. There's no mass of dialogue and the system breeds confidence to try more complex tasks and procedures

Me
Tap this button to see your own location. You'll need to be connected to the internet either through Wi-Fi or using a 3G sim, if you are a 3G iPad owner

Map Type
Here we are using a standard Map but you can use a satellite image, or a hybrid that shows satellite imagery overlaid with map info like road and place names

Where it's at
Once you've tapped the current location button your location will appear as a blue dot with a blue ring around it

Pick a Pin
Tap on any pin and you will see an information window which will allow you to share the location with anyone you like

Knowledge base

VCF file

'.vcf' is the extension of a file used to store electronic business cards in the vCard format. A 'vcf' file may contain name and address info, phone numbers, email addresses, URLs, logos, photos, and audio clips. 'vcf' or vCard format is popular to share contact info on the internet or between devices. Other standards for sharing contact info is hCard and Internet Business Card.

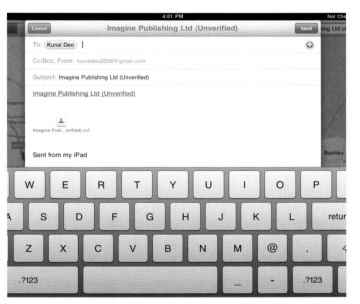

03 Sending the location

Type in the email address of the person you want to share your location with. Email is already populated with important information such as the location (in the form of a 'vcf' file) and the location's name as the subject and body. Tap Send to send the location to the recipient.

04 Using the Shared Location

Open the email with the 'vcf' file attached in it. Tap on it to open the information pop-up. It is similar to one you have seen in the Maps application, but it contains more information. It also contains the Map URL. Tap on Map URL to launch the Maps app with the sent address.

Getting started

Access video content via the YouTube app

You don't need us to explain what YouTube is, but it will be useful to know how to get the most out of it on your iPad. It works using 3G and Wi-Fi

The built-in YouTube iPad app is a lesson in thoughtful design, and manages to bring the desktop experience to a mobile device while maintaining all of the functionality of the main web portal YouTube uses. With a YouTube account in place you can save favourites, share videos with friends and comment on videos you like, and your changes will be accessible on your desktop automatically. It all sounds very simple and on the whole it is, but some pointers will help you to get even more out of the experience.

It is worth remembering that, should you use the service on a 3G iPad, you will be pushing a hefty amount of data so be aware of the limits your network provider has imposed on your account. Wi-Fi is the recommended solution for YouTube-use on an iPad because it speeds up the loading of videos and also makes the experience feel more like the one you have come to expect on a desktop. The iPad YouTube app really does bring every feature to your mobile life, and here we will show you how to get up and running in no time and how to make the most of its potential. It's all free so you have no reason not to try it for yourself.

YouTube Make the most of YouTube

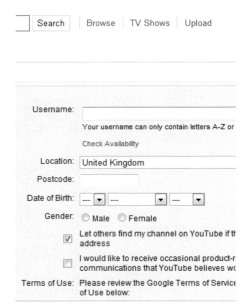

01 Getting started
To utilise every feature in YouTube for the iPad you will need an account. Go to **www.youtube. com** and click the Create Account option in the top right-hand corner.

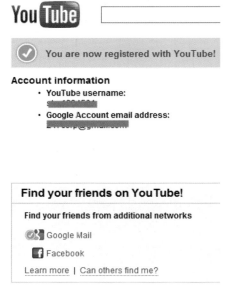

02 Create an account
Complete the requested information and then set up a new Google account (or use your current account in the next page). This completes the process for setting up a new YouTube account.

03 Make YouTube personal
On the iPad, open the YouTube app and tap Favourites, then tap the Sign In icon, and input your username and password. You will now have access to your videos, favourites and more.

YouTube on iPad

Once you discover how to use YouTube on your iPad, you may decide to use it as a replacement for the desktop version…

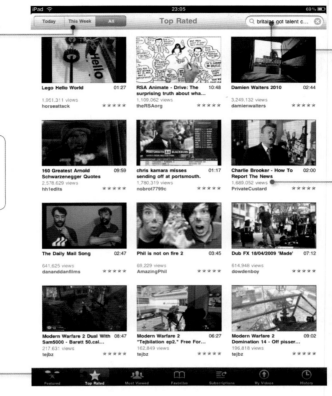

Popular videos
The most recent popular videos of all time, from the past week and from today are a useful way to simply browse and see what's happening on YouTube

Keep it personal
Your main account information is kept up to date and is accessible via the handy icons at the bottom of each section

Search everything
You can search almost the entire YouTube database from your iPad in the same way you use a standard web search engine

Previews
Each video is previewed with an icon, rating and the number of views, which together should tell you if it's worth watching

Knowledge base

Streaming

Streaming video wirelessly is very bandwidth-hungry, and overuse on 3G alone could cause you to break the limit on your data account. Your network provider is then within its rights to send you a warning. If possible, try to use Wi-Fi because this will not only perform better, but could potentially save you a lot of money.

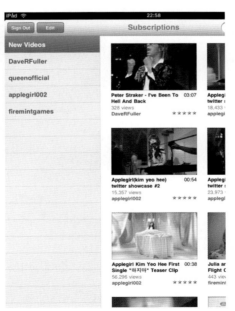

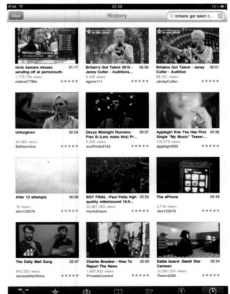

04 Explore the content

You can now explore the content within YouTube. When you tap a video to watch it you will see a selection of icons at the top of the screen that you can use to mark favourites or share videos.

05 Fully in step

Any changes that you make to your YouTube account on the iPad will be mirrored on your desktop, and vice versa, so you can use both and keep the changes intact.

06 Keep track

YouTube includes a history icon (found along the bottom of the screen) that shows your most recently viewed videos. This is useful if you forget to add a viewed video to your favourites list.

Getting started

Using the camera connection kit

With this bit of kit, you can now view photos on the iPad without loading them to a computer first. Here's how…

While the iPad isn't a computer in its own right – you still need another computer to activate and sync with it – Apple has taken steps to add some much needed functionality so you're not totally dependent on a second machine. One of these was to introduce a camera connection kit, which allows users to directly import photographs from a camera or SD card. This way, users can view their snaps on the iPad without going through the hassle of loading them on a Mac or PC and then syncing them through iTunes.

As you would expect, the process is typically simple once you've actually bought the connection kit and you can have your pictures up and running on the iPad in a matter of minutes. The iPad will instantly recognise that you have connected a camera kit and will open the Photos app ready for you to start the import. Camera connection kits are available from **www.apple.com** and all good official resellers. In this tutorial, we walk you through using this bit of kit with your iPad.

Photos Get your snaps on the iPad

01 Get connected

Once you've connected the kit to the dock the Photos app opens and you can see all the photos on the memory card. A new tab will have appeared at the top of the Photos app called Camera.

02 Tap to tick

You can import all of the photos in one go if you like or you can tap on pictures to import them individually. Each picture you tap on will show a blue and white tick box.

Picture perfect

Working your way around
the import process

Tab clue
The tab at the top will alter when
you connect the camera. This is
the only way to see if the kit is
connected correctly to your iPad

Top tiles
Like all the other pictures on your
iPad those about to be imported
appear in the classic tile system,
allowing you to flick up and down
through them before you import

Stop it
If you realise you've made a mistake
you can always tap the Stop Import
button to halt the process

Import times
The file transfer will be pretty quick
for most files. Video and very large
images will obviously take a little
bit longer

Knowledge base

Cards
There are two types of connection
kit for the iPad. One will allow you
to connect your camera directly
using the USB lead it comes with,
much the same way you connect to
your computer. The other lets you
connect an SD card like you would
with a standard SD reader.

03 Import choice
Tap the Import button on the top right-hand side of the interface and you
will be presented with two options. Simply tap the one that suits you best
– Import All or Import Selected.

04 Nice notice
Once the import is complete a dialogue box will appear offering you the
choice of whether to delete or keep the picture you have imported. Tap the
one that suits you best.

Create a slideshow on the iPad

Show your best pictures off with a cool slideshow, complete with transitions and your own music

Apple has taken a lot of time over the Photos app on the iPad. We know this because it's a completely different app to the one that appears on the iPhone, even though they both share the same operating system. One of the things that sets this new Photos app apart is its ability to show incredible picture slideshows, with far more control than the iPhone equivalent. A large part of this is, of course, down to the larger screen with greater resolution, but another part is the way the interface is so easy to use that you'll really enjoy creating and watching them with friends. Once you've learned how to create a slideshow, we're confident that you'll be so impressed that you'll be making them all the time. The real shame is that, unlike the desktop version in iPhoto, you can't save the results and share them with others. For now, though, just enjoy the brilliance of these slideshows.

"iPad's Photos can show picture slideshows with far more control than the iPhone equivalent"

Photos Setting up a slideshow

01 Load it, tap it

Load the Photos app from your home screen and then navigate to an album or a picture that you like. Then tap the 'Slideshow' button at the top of the interface to begin.

02 Options

The options window will now appear and you can begin to customise your slideshow. Tap on the transition you wish to use between photos. You have the choice of five different ones.

03 Tune it

You can add music to the slideshow by tapping the music button. This will bring up all of your songs that have been synced from iTunes, so if you want a specific song make sure it's on there.

The iPad slideshow interface

Be amazed at how simply you can create a beautiful slideshow

Transitions
Origami is a new Apple transition type and it basically looks as though photos are folding out from under each other. Very cool

Pop-ups
Having windows within windows makes navigation on the iPad a complete joy. You pretty much always stay on the same page

Scrubber
The Photos app has a cool and very easy to use scrubber at the bottom of the interface, so you can navigate through a large number of pictures very easily

Rotation
As you would expect, the photos will auto-rotate when the iPad is itself rotated. This way you can get the most from both portrait and landscape pictures

Knowledge base
Sounds
The integration of music into the slideshow adds a whole new dimension to watching your pictures. Your music can really set the mood. It is possible to create a playlist from the iPod app on the iPad, so you can create something specific on the fly.

04 Playlist it
If you are really organised you will have already created a custom playlist for the slideshow and can use this now. Tap on whatever you wish to use to select it and you're just about ready to go.

05 Ready, steady
Once you have everything in place, just tap the 'Start Slideshow' button at the bottom of the 'Slideshow Options' window. Your slideshow will begin immediately with your chosen settings.

06 Watch in awe
You can now relax with the iPad, watching your favourite pictures from your most recent holiday or event and listening to your favourite tunes while you do it. It's as simple as that.

Getting started

Set up a photo frame using your iPad

The iPad is a great touch screen computer, but when it's not in use you can use it as a photo frame. Here's how…

It's this kind of functionality and thought that makes Apple the great company that it is. We can imagine the meeting where the people are discussing the iPad and someone chimes in that it should be able to be used as a photo frame, and someone just says, 'Okay, we'll do that' – and then they make it happen and make it awesome. When you're not using it – which will be hardly ever, unless you're asleep – the iPad can become a very cool photo frame. It takes a few steps to set up, but once it's done you simply tap a button on the lock screen and the photos will start playing. In typical Apple fashion, you can assign transitions and pick which photos you want the iPad to display. If you have a particular album that you'd like to add to the iPad, you'll need to sync it to the device using iTunes or by using the camera connection kit (see page 74).

> ## "It takes a few steps to set up, but once it's done you simply tap a button on the lock screen and the photos will start playing"

Photos Set up a photo frame

01 Passcode
Tap the settings icon on the home screen and then tap on General and then Passcode. If your passcode is already set up you'll have to enter it to edit the settings in this section.

02 Picture frame
Tap the Picture Frame button so that it moves to on. To make changes to the behaviour of this functionality, tap on the Picture Frame menu above General in the left-hand pane.

03 Lots of options
Here you can change the transition, tell the iPad to zoom in on faces that it detects in the images, shuffle the pictures, and change which pictures are used in the photo frame.

Customising your photo frame

The iPad offers almost as many settings as a dedicated frame

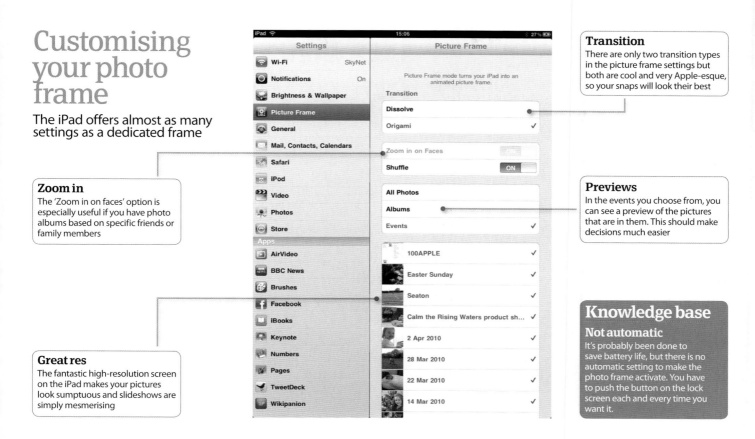

Zoom in
The 'Zoom in on faces' option is especially useful if you have photo albums based on specific friends or family members

Great res
The fantastic high-resolution screen on the iPad makes your pictures look sumptuous and slideshows are simply mesmerising

Transition
There are only two transition types in the picture frame settings but both are cool and very Apple-esque, so your snaps will look their best

Previews
In the events you choose from, you can see a preview of the pictures that are in them. This should make decisions much easier

Knowledge base

Not automatic
It's probably been done to save battery life, but there is no automatic setting to make the photo frame activate. You have to push the button on the lock screen each and every time you want it.

04 Lots of ticks
Tap on the Events section to see all the events that you have added to the iPad. From here, you can tick the ones you want the iPad to display when in photo frame mode.

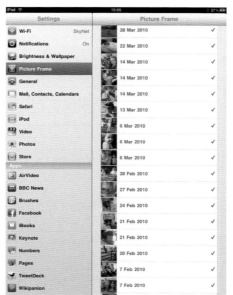

05 Flick it
No matter how many events you have catalogued in picture form on the iPad, you can easily flick up and down through them without ever leaving the main settings screen.

06 From the lock
Now, once the screen is locked, you'll have the option to tap the photo frame button next to the lock slider. Once tapped your photos will begin to display until you tell it to stop.

Getting started

Get the most out of iPad videos

The iPad is perfectly designed for the mobile movie experience thanks to its large screen, long battery life and carry-anywhere form. It's time to make the most of it…

The Video feature alone has the potential to keep you occupied on long plane journeys, in hotels or waiting rooms, and adds a use to the iPad that could justify half of the cost straight away. It has been designed for ease of use, as most Apple software is, and takes care of many of the niggles found in competing devices. For example, it will automatically play a film from the point you left it, and expanding the screen requires a simple double tap. Everything is designed to help you get the most from the experience, but some tips are still useful to get you off to a flying start. In this step-by-step we will show you how to obtain new movies, how to transfer them to your iPad and how to make the most of the viewing experience. You could easily do all of this yourself, but a little knowledge goes a long way and missing out on the movie capabilities of the iPad would be a real shame given the benefits it offers.

> "The Video feature alone adds a use to the iPad that could justify half of the cost straight away"

iPad Videos Make the most of movies

01 Grab a film

The easiest way to obtain good quality content is via iTunes. Navigate to the Films or TV Programmes section and choose the film you would like to rent or buy. You can also try some free trailers to get started without spending any money.

02 Put it on the iPad

The most stable method of moving films to your iPad is to choose 'Manually manage music and video' in the iPad summary screen in iTunes. You can then just drag new films over to your iPad in the left-hand column when you want to.

Watch movies on your iPad

Get the most out of the Videos app

Full screen
Tapping on this icon will alternate between full-screen and widescreen viewing. You can also double tap anywhere on screen to achieve this effect

Full control
You can move to specific parts of a video by moving the slider at the top with your finger; the further down the screen your finger is, the more precise the movement

Back where you left off
Videos automatically remembers where you finished watching and will start any film at that exact place when you open it up again

Main controls
The main control keys are standard and are brought up by tapping the screen once. You can play, pause, forward or rewind when you need to

Knowledge base

HD
Many iTunes movies and TV programmes are now offered in HD format, which offers a much crisper viewing experience. Sometimes you will pay more for the video, but think of it in a similar way to paying more for Blu-ray. These files will also be larger in size, sometimes significantly, so make sure you have adequate space before you buy.

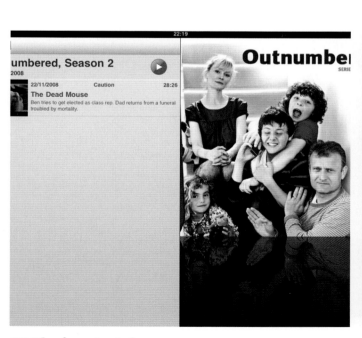

03 The fun starts here
All you need to do now is simply click the Videos icon and choose the film you want to watch from the list of videos that you have installed on your iPad. The film (or TV programme, for that matter) will immediately start to play from the beginning.

04 Small changes
Double-tapping the screen will make the movie play in full-screen mode, and doing so again will take it back to standard format (which is useful for widescreen films). The rest of the on-screen tweaks are obvious in their implementation, such as play, pause, etc.

Easily create a song playlist using the iPod app

Manipulate a desktop-sized iPod and have your favourite tracks at your fingertips

With all the bells and whistles that the iPad has to offer, it's easy to forget that it's also a very impressive iPod. In fact we're not sure whether the app should be called iPod but rather iTunes, as it resembles the desktop app much more than it does any of the versions on any iPod or the iPhone. The interface is clean, simple, easy to manipulate and great fun to play with. The familiarity to iTunes doesn't just extent to the app's looks either. The functionality is also pretty similar – the key difference being the way you access and change information. It's all done with a finger and for that reason it feels a thousand times more intimate than using the desktop version.

One of the first things you may want to do on the iPad's iPod is create a playlist. The system Apple has devised for this is really impressive. So impressive, and fun, that you'll want to sift through an entire library and create one playlist after another. Here's how…

> "The interface is clean, simple, easy to manipulate and great fun to play with"

iPod Create a playlist

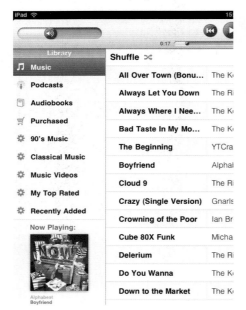

01 Open and tap plus
Open the iPod on your iPad and set the iPad to the landscape mode. Now tap the + button in the bottom-left corner of the screen to begin creating a brand-new playlist.

02 Type the title
An iPhone-style blue window appears allowing you to name the playlist. The near full-size keyboard also springs up from the bottom of the app, allowing you to easily type in a suitable title.

03 Save it
Give your playlist an appropriate name and then tap the Save button. The playlist will then appear in the left-hand panel of the iPod and a brand-new screen will appear.

Music while you're mobile

Setting up playlists on the iPad is a breeze

Easy edit
Apple has made the editing process for playlists very simple indeed. You can drag items up and down or remove them completely by tapping on the red 'Stop' buttons on the left of every song or playlist

Familiar favourites
Here you'll find the sections that appear in regular iTunes that give you instant access to music videos, top-rated tunes, recently added tracks and recently or most played songs

Handy buttons
On the left of the interface are two of the most useful buttons on the iPod. The 'plus' sign lets you create playlists and the other button allows you to create Genius playlists

Bottom tabs
The iPad's iPod has tabs at the bottom for you to alter the view you get when looking at your library. Tap on them to activate

Knowledge base

Sync it
If you want to add songs from your computer's library you'll need to sync your songs with the iPad, otherwise you can purchase songs from the mobile iTunes store and they will be added to your iPad's iPod – these can then be synced back to your computer if you wish.

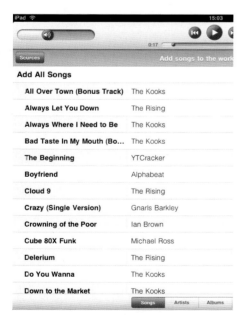

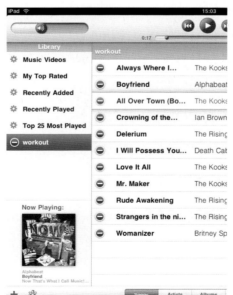

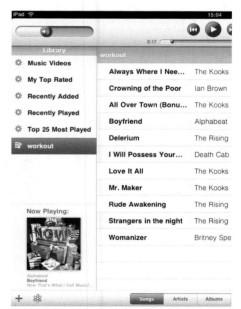

04 Tap it out
Your whole library now appears in the main window and you can tap on each song you wish to appear in the library. Selected items get greyed out so you don't pick them twice.

05 Done, drag, Done
Once you've picked your songs hit Done to see another screen. This time you can drag tunes into the order you want them by dragging up the lined symbol on the right of each song.

06 Play it, love it
When you're completely set on the order that you want, all you have to do is hit the Done button again and your playlist is ready to play and enjoy at your leisure.

Use iTunes on the iPad

You can download all your favourite movies and music from iTunes without needing to connect it to your computer

Being able to download music and movies on the go is one of the best things about the iPad. With the enormous selection available on the iTunes Store, you're unlikely to be lost for something to suit your mood. It's not just music and movies though, as you can also download TV programmes, audio books and podcasts. There's even the iTunes U section, which is full of education resources.

Your purchases are automatically synced and backed up to your copy of iTunes on your computer whenever you connect the iPad to it. This means that you'll be able to watch your movies on your computer or Apple TV and, more importantly, that you'll have a guaranteed backup of everything you purchase.

To use iTunes on the iPad you'll need an account to get going, but once that's set up you can buy songs, apps or movies wherever you are. All you need is a credit card (or, failing that, some iTunes gift cards).

"Being able to download music and movies on the go is one of the best things about the iPad"

Navigate the iTunes Store on your iPad

Download direct to your device

Search
Find everything you're after by tapping in the search box and typing. iTunes will automatically suggest what it thinks you're after. To select one, just tap it

Featured, Charts, Genius
To see what the bestselling items are tap on the Top Charts button, or to see suggestions based on your purchasing history and iTunes library tap Genius

Latest content
The very latest releases and some of the more popular content is automatically displayed. You can see more by tapping on the arrows at each corner of the section

Easy access
To get to a specific section quickly simply tap on the relevant icon along the bottom of the screen. This narrows down the amount of searching you have to do

iTunes Make the most of iTunes on iPad

01 Buy music, movies and more

To buy music and video from the iTunes Store you'll need to set up an account. Simply tap on an item to buy it and choose Create New Account.

02 Agree to the terms and conditions that appear

There are a few steps to opening a new account on the iPad. Once you've tapped to confirm your location you'll then be offered the terms and conditions for using the account.

03 Credit card details

You'll need to provide your credit card details. If you don't want to do this, simply buy an iTunes gift card and enter the number here.

04 Search

To search for your favourite music, video and television programmes, tap in the search box. The on-screen keyboard will appear so you can type your entry.

05 Music, Video, TV

To see what's just been added or the latest promotions, just tap on the Music, Films and TV Programmes icons along the bottom of the screen.

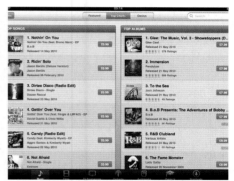

06 Charts

The most popular content in each of the sections is on the Charts page. There are charts pages for everything, including podcasts, video, television and music.

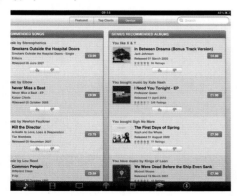

07 Genius

If you have bought from the Store before, tap on the Genius button to see recommendations based on the content of your library.

08 Other offers

On the main screen it's easy to be lured in by the flashy graphics, but scroll down and you'll see further offers like free content and cheap music.

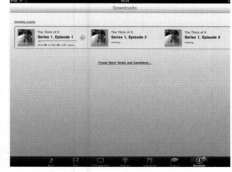

09 Monitor downloads

When you've made a purchase in iTunes you can see how long it's likely going to take by tapping on the Downloads icon in the bottom-right of the screen.

Use iTunes to get music

Preview and download your favourite songs from Apple's iTunes Store using your iPad's iTunes app and then enjoy music on the move!

You could link your iPad to your desktop computer and transfer your favourite songs onto it via iTunes. However, as you're likely to carry your precious iPad around wherever you go (hopefully in a soft protective case to keep it in pristine condition!), you have the freedom to browse, download and store your favourite music tracks onto it, so that you can listen to them whenever (and wherever) you fancy. You no longer need to be chained to a home computer thanks to the iPad's own iTunes app. When you take a fancy to a song that you hear in your local Wi-Fi enabled coffee shop (or using a 3G enable iPad) you can fire up iTunes on the iPad, search for the song on the iTunes Store and download it there and then to expand your music collection. You will need to create an account with the iTunes Store before you can buy and download music to your iPad, though.

> "You no longer need to be chained to a home computer thanks to the iPad's own iTunes app"

iTunes   Download music from iTunes

01 Open iTunes

Click on the iTunes app on your iPad to launch it. It will take you to the iTunes Store. Tap on the note-shaped Music icon at the bottom left of the page. You'll see thumbnails linking to new and noteworthy music tracks, as well as colourful banners advertising new albums.

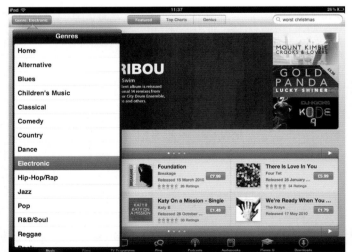

02 Choose a genre

To find the type of music you enjoy, click on Genres at the top left of the screen. This lets you fine-tune your browsing to Pop or Electronic music for example. Click on a genre to access its page. You can then tap the left/right arrows to scroll through various thumbnails.

Get music from iTunes

Browse, preview and download music using iTunes' very easy to use interface

Preview
Hear a sample of each audio track by clicking on this adjacent icon. This is the best way to get a flavour of the album's contents

Ratings
Get an instant idea about how good (or bad!) an album is by checking out the ratings it received from previous customers

Purchase
If you're only after a single track you can download it for £0.99 by clicking here, though some tracks are only available when you buy the entire album

Handy thumbnails
Thumbnails of album covers help you browse multiple albums more quickly. Click on a thumbnail for more detailed information about the album's contents

Knowledge base

Transfer purchases

Once you've downloaded an album (or track) directly onto your iPad, it makes sense to back it up onto your home computer. Plug your iPad into the desktop computer and fire up its copy of iTunes. The iPad will appear under Devices at the left of the iTunes screen. Go to File and choose Transfer purchases from iPad. iTunes will then search for any music downloaded onto the iPad and copy it into your desktop computer's Library. You can now enjoy your iPad purchased music on the move, or from the comfort of your own home.

03 Preview a track

Type a favourite Artist or Title into the search field at the top-right corner. A variety of thumbnail links will appear. To discover more about a particular album click on its Thumbnail. Clicking a track name will play you a preview. Customer ratings and reviews will help you make an informed choice.

04 Buy and download

To buy a song, click on the price button on the right. To buy the whole album click the album's price button, then click Buy Album. Enter your Apple ID Password so that iTunes can take your payment. The desired song or album will then be downloaded to your iPad.

Getting started

Use iTunes to get movies

Discover recent Hollywood blockbusters by browsing Apple's iTunes Store via your iPad, then download and enjoy the movies on the move!

The iPad is the perfect way to enjoy a movie on the move (or tucked up in bed!) thanks to its generously sized screen. If you've got it connected to a Wi-Fi network you can browse a wide selection of new and classic movies via the iPad's iTunes app, then download them to rent or keep. Indeed, renting a film via the iPad couldn't be more convenient or easy, as it saves you the time and effort of driving to the local rental store. You don't need to worry about being fined for returning it your film later either, as the movie simply becomes unavailable 48 hours after you start watching it.

If you use your iPad to buy a movie to boost your digital film collection, you can transfer it to your desktop computer after you've watched it, so it won't permanently hog valuable space on your iPad. You can always pop the film back on the iPad at a later date if you fancy watching it on a long train journey.

"You can transfer the film to your computer, so it won't hog valuable space on your iPad"

iTunes Downloading a movie

01 Open iTunes on iPad

Click on the iTunes app to launch it. It will take you to the iTunes Store's homepage. Tap on the filmstrip 'Films' icon at the bottom left of the screen. You'll see thumbnails linking to new and noteworthy movies, as well as colourful banners advertising the latest film releases.

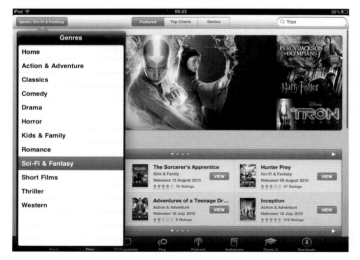

02 Browse a genre

To find the type of film you enjoy, click on Genres at the top left of the homepage. This lets you fine-tune your browsing to Sci-Fi & Fantasy or Drama, for example. Click on a genre to access its page. You can then tap the left/right arrows to scroll through various thumbnails.

Get movies from iTunes

Browse by genre then rent or buy a movie to enjoy on your iPad

Rental
When you rent a movie via iTunes you can wait up to 30 days before you decide to watch it. This gives you the freedom to enjoy the film when it suits you

Charts
Instead of browsing by Genre, you can see what's hot by clicking on the Top Charts button. This should give you some inspiration about what to watch

Format
High-definition movies are also available to rent or buy. They will take up more space on you iPad, however, and are more expensive than the standard definition version

Terrific trailers
Click here to get a flavour of a movie before coughing up your hard-earned cash. This will fill your iPad's screen with a QuickTime trailer for the film

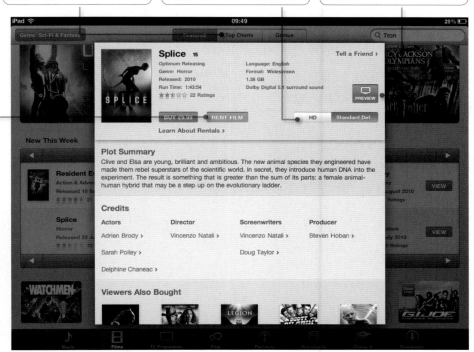

Knowledge base
Resolution
Full HD movies have a screen size (or resolution) of 1080 horizontal lines. The iPad's screen consists of 768 horizontal lines, so it won't display as much detail as a dedicated HD TV screen. This is why it makes sense to download movies from the iTunes Store in the cheaper standard definition (SD) format. To rent an HD version of a movie can cost you a pound more than the cost of the SD version. You can put the money you save towards a bag of popcorn instead!

03 Read reviews
Click on a thumbnail to discover more about a particular movie. Scroll down to read some iTunes customer reviews, as this will help you decide if the film is worth buying, renting or avoiding. You can use the Sort By pop-up menu to see the most helpful, most recent or even most critical reviews.

04 HD or not HD?
You can download movies in high definition (HD) or standard definition, but you do have to pay more to see your download in the high definition format. To make your selection, simply click on the appropriate icon before buying your film.

Use iTunes to get TV programmes

Download TV programmes using the iPad's iTunes app

Thanks to gadgets like hard drive recorders that are built into many Freeview boxes, we're used to recording our favourite shows so we can watch them whenever we want to. This frees us from having to sit in front of the telly at specific times, so we can tailor our viewing schedule around more important things.

If you forget to set your machine to record a particular show, then it's a simple matter of hunting it down on the iTunes Store and downloading it straight to your iPad. This means you're free to watch what you want, wherever you want. You can turn boring commuting time into a more productive TV catch-up session. The iTunes Store is also packed with classic television shows, so you can take a trip down memory lane or discover old programmes you missed the first time round. Here's how to find and download your favourite TV shows straight to the iPad.

> "The Store is also packed with classic television shows, so you can take a trip down memory lane"

iTunes Find the TV shows you want

01 Open iTunes on iPad

Click on the iTunes app to launch it. It will take you to the iTunes Store's homepage. Tap on the Television icon in the bar at the bottom of the screen. You'll see thumbnails linking to new or noteworthy TV shows, as well as colourful banners advertising the latest releases.

02 Search for a show

Click on Genres at the top left of the homepage to narrow down your search to Comedy or Drama, for example. Click on a genre to access its page. By clicking on Top Charts you can see what's new or popular, or you can type a specific show's title into the search field.

TV on iTunes

Download an episode (or entire series) and enjoy TV on your iPad

Format
Many modern TV shows like Matt Smith's era of *Doctor Who* are shot in high definition, though you can download the same shows in the cheaper standard definition format too

Fab Freebies
Many TV shows promote themselves by giving you free content. This can be anything from a short trailer to a longer featurette. Click on a button to download the free clip straight to your iPad

Downloads
You can see how many TV Programmes are currently downloading by looking here. Click on this icon to see the progress of your downloads. You can then watch the show in your Videos app

Terrific trailers
Click here to get a preview of a particular episode to help you decide whether to purchase it or not. This will fill your iPad's screen with a QuickTime trailer for the TV show

03 Preview a clip

A search result might list a range of different series and episodes, especially on long-running shows like *Doctor Who*. Click View to discover more about a particular series. You can then preview individual episodes by clicking on the thumbnail to their left. Preview clips run for 30 seconds.

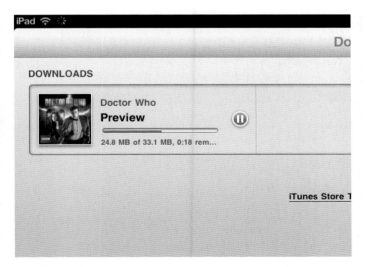

04 Download

You can download individual episodes or buy the entire series in a click. Buying the series as a whole is usually much cheaper than buying individual episodes, so decide up front if you want to own the lot! Click the appropriate Buy icon to start the download process then enjoy the show.

Create and save Genius playlists on your iPad

Creating your own special playlists is great but by letting the iPad do all the hard work you can get some really cool musical mixes

Keeping track of all the music on your iPad can be a bit of a pain. It's surprising how much music you can fit onto even just the 16GB version. With all that music it makes sense to keep track of it all and to create playlists.

Of course, listening to whole albums is fine, but then we all have our favourite tracks and like to hear them more often than others. Creating playlists manually is a great way of doing this, but it's time consuming and if you don't keep them updated they soon get tiresome.

You could just stick your whole music collection on random, but even this throws up issues like those hidden tracks or fillers that ruin a smooth transition, or the odd song you're bored of hearing. The best solution may well be Genius mixes.

Apple has created a tool that lets you select a track and automatically create a playlist of music that complements each other. It's a great way of keeping the music going around a certain theme and in the main it's incredibly reliable.

iPod Make Genius mixes on the iPad

01 Open iPod

Fire up your iPad and then launch the iPod applications. Tap on Music at the top-left of the Library column. Scroll down until you find a song that would make a good foundation for your playlist; this will be the basis of your list so make sure you pick something good!

02 Make a Genius mix

When you have found a track that most suits your current mood, tap on it to start it playing. When you're ready, tap on the Genius symbol that you can find tucked away at the bottom-left of the screen, next to the + symbol.

Playlists on the iPad

Create your own Genius playlist

Library
All of your playlists are shown here and each Genius mix is named after the first track you use to make the playlist. To start your playlist tap on it and then on the top track

Delete a playlist
If you get bored with a playlist or have too many to comfortably use your library then you can delete it very easily. Tap on the playlist and then tap on Delete to get rid of the Genius mix

Views
To view your music collection in any of five different views simply tap on one of the five options. Making Genius mixes is much simpler if you view your music as Songs, however

Genius mix
The Genius mix icon can be used at any time to make a new playlist, even from existing Genius playlists. Simply tap it to create a playlist based on the currently playing track

Knowledge base
Genius mixes
Contrary to what you might think, Genius mixes aren't just randomly thrown together and Apple is working behind the scenes to make the music fit. iTunes assesses your music collection and from an extensive database puts together the tracks that go together best

03 Asses your mix
You'll see that a new playlist called Genius has been added to your library and that songs have already been populated to it. If you don't like the tracks simply tap on Refresh, or if you'd prefer to choose a different starting point tap New.

04 Save your playlist
Once you are happy with the tracks that are on your playlist all you have to do is click on Save. The playlist that was called Genius is now renamed to the starting track of your Genius mix. By default a Genius mix contains 25 tracks.

Use the App Store on your iPad

One of the best things about your iPad is that it can be upgraded on the go. The App Store allows you to make the iPad even more magical than it already is…

The iPad is (as Steve Jobs says) magical, and a major part of the magic is that you can expand its capabilities with cheap or even free apps. The App Store has been a roaring success for Apple, with over 200,000 applications to choose from – not to mention the 1 billion Dollars that it's made for developers.

The number and range of applications on offer is quite stunning. The App Store has applications to help you plan large projects, word processors, web browsers; the list is endless. The software tends to be incredibly good value too – it's amazing what your iPad can do with just a 59p investment. The fact that the App Store is right there on your iPad means that you can buy stuff on the go, too, and download apps directly onto the device.

With so much choice it can be quite difficult to discover exactly what you want, but the App Store on the iPad is easy enough to use when you know how, so follow these simple steps to learn more…

"There are apps to help you plan large projects, word processors, web browsers; the list is endless"

Navigate the App Store on your iPad

Find and download iPad apps

Search
Find exactly what you need by tapping in the search box and typing. Suggestions will automatically drop-down as you type – simply tap on them to jump to those results

Latest apps
Find out what applications have just hit the App Store by tapping on the Release Date button. This will show you the very latest approved apps

Featured
The default screen on the App Store shows off some of the best applications available in a Cover Flow style – simply swipe left and right to see what's there

Navigation
Get to the charts and categories sections here by tapping on the relevant icons. If Updates has a red icon with a number in it, upgrades are ready to be downloaded

App Store   Learn how to use the App Store on your iPad

01 Getting started

Once you've set up an account, simply tap the App Store icon to get started. The first screen you see has some of the most interesting apps as defined by Apple.

02 Staff Picks

If you'd like to see what the staff at Apple are interested in and using the most, scroll down with a swipe to the Staff Favorites. Tap See All to view them all.

03 App of the week

Each week a new app is chosen to be the app of the week. These are often surprising and it's a great way to find a really good app you might not have seen.

04 Find apps

If you know the name of the app you want, simply tap in the search field and type it there. If you're not sure just put the type of application to find what you need.

05 Charts

Apple lets you see the top ten selling apps and the top ten free ones. Simply tap on the Top Charts button at the bottom of the screen to see what they are.

06 What's hot

The What's Hot section lists some of the best apps that might not have made it to the charts or have been featured yet. Tap What's Hot at the top of the Store.

07 Categories

If you're not sure what you want but have a general idea, tap the Categories button. This shows twenty different groups for apps to narrow down your choice.

08 Buying an app

When you're ready to buy an app, getting it is really simple. Tap on the price and it will change to 'Buy App'. Tap again and then enter your account password.

09 Updating an app

Over time, and more regularly than you might imagine, apps will be updated. Tap on Updates and then either Update All or pick applications to update individually.

Download iBooks from the App Store

iBooks is your one-stop shop for all the latest releases and free, out-of-copyright titles. Here's how to get it from the App Store

If you like reading on your iPad then you really need to get hold of iBooks. It's an app for all the titles you've downloaded and also a book store where you can buy new and popular books from all the leading publishers. There are also free titles like the *iPad User Guide* and out-of-copyright classics like *Treasure Island* and *The Art Of War*.

The interface is split into two sections: one is the bookshelf for all your titles, and the other is the store. To read your books you simply tap on them on the bookshelf. Before you do all that though you need to get the iBooks app onto your iPad, and this really is a very simple process indeed. If you are away from your computer with iTunes installed and want to get iBooks and download it directly to your iPad, you're in the right place. We guide you through with some simple steps that will get you reading digitally in not time at all.

> "It's a book store where you can buy new and popular books from all the leading publishers"

App Store Download the iBooks app

01 Go to the App Store

The first step is to turn your iPad on and make sure you are connected to the internet. If you aren't then there's unfortunately no way that this can work. On the favourites bar at the bottom of the screen is the App Store icon. Tap on it.

02 Using the Store

With a live internet connection the App Store will appear displaying all the latest titles in a variety of categories. The currently promoted apps appear at the top of the page. To save looking for the iBooks app we simply need to use the Search function.

Installing the application

Discover everything about the latest version of the iBooks app

More information

If you tap on the iBooks icon in the App Store you get a more detailed page of information about it and can also download it here as well

Latest information

Apps get updated all the time and iBooks is no exception. Under the What's New heading will be details of the improvements since the last version of the app

If all else fails

If the installation doesn't work for some reason then you can report the problem to Apple from this page. Tap on Report a Problem and let them know

Install the app

Tap on the word 'Free' under the icon for the app and it turns into 'Install App'. Tap on this to download and install it

Knowledge base

Copyright and books

Copyright law is different from country to country, though the EU has tried to standardise it across the European Union. Many countries have signed up to the Berne Convention, and in those, any author is automatically granted copyright to their work without having to register it. Copyright, however, doesn't last forever and in most cases it ceases either 50 or 70 years after the death of the author. That's why there are classic novels available on iBooks for free. The copyright on them has lapsed and they can be reprinted or republished.

(iBooks App Store screenshot)

iPad ᐧ 14:20 Not Charging

Search | iBooks | iBooks

iBooks

Apple Inc.
iBooks

INSTALL APP

Category: Books
Updated: 15 December 2010
Current Version: 1.2
Size: 15.2 MB
Languages: English, Chinese, ...
Developer: Apple Inc.
© 2010

Rated 4+

Requirements:
Compatible with iPhone, iPod touch and iPad.
Requires iOS 3.2 or later.

Developer Web Site

App Support

Application Licence Agreement

Developer Page ›
Tell A Friend ›
Report a Problem ›

Description

iBooks is an amazing way to download and read books. iBooks includes the iBookstore, where you can download the latest best-selling books or your favorite classics – day or night. Browse your library on a beautiful bookshelf, tap a book to open it, flip through pages with a swipe or a tap, and bookmark or add notes to your favorite passages.

Features:....   More ▼

What's New in Version 1.2   Updated 15 December 2010

- Experience fully illustrated books, from children's picture books to beautifully designed art books, available for download in the iBookstore.
- Organize your books and PDFs into personal Collections. Swipe left or right to jump between Collections.
- Print PDF documents and notes you've written in iBooks using AirPrint.
- iBooks now fits more words per page by automatically hyphenating text, available only on iOS 4.2 or later.   More ▼

03 Search for iBooks

Tap on the Search bar on the top right of the App Store screen. Type the word 'iBooks' with the keyboard. As soon as you start, the full word may appear in the Suggestions box. Either finish typing or tap on the suggested word. Tap Search on the keyboard.

04 Install the app

Under the iPad Apps results, the first one will be iBooks. To install it tap on the word 'Free' next to the icon. This changes to 'Install App'. Tap on that and you will be prompted for your iTunes password. Enter it and iBooks will begin downloading.

Getting started

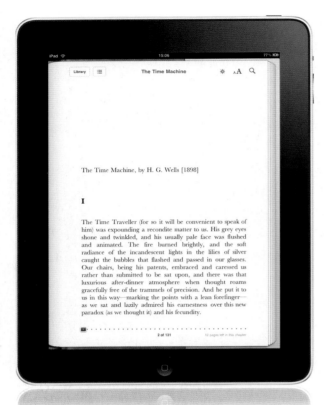

Purchase an iBook

Learn how to buy an iBook and open up to a whole world of digital reading

One of the reasons for the iPad's existence is to take on Amazon's Kindle. It's very easy to get lost in a world of crazy apps, accelerometers and multi-touch gestures, but the iPad was conceived to be a fantastic eBook reader. It obviously has a number of advantages over the Kindle in that it can do a great deal more than a dedicated device, but on a purely eBook-reading scale, the iPad is still one of the most advanced out there. What's more is that Apple already has a tried and tested way to deliver eBooks directly to its device: namely the iTunes Store. Apple hasn't just bundled the new books into that system, though, because it's created a separate space for these so that users can be sure of what they are downloading.

Once you have downloaded the app (see the previous tutorial), iBooks holds all of your eBooks, and from there you can access the custom-built iBooks Store to make purchases, which get downloaded directly. The system is magnificent in its simplicity and, like the App Store, it makes impulse buys a regular occurrence. This tutorial will take you through your first download from iBooks so that you can get a feel for the system. It's then up to you to resist buying a library's worth of content on each visit!

> "The iBooks system is magnificent in its simplicity, making impulse buys a regular occurrence"

iBooks Purchase a book

01 Load and launch
You have to download iBooks from the App Store and then, once it's loaded, have a look at the free copy of *Winnie The Pooh*. To purchase your first book, hit the Store button on the top left.

02 Familiar feel
The iBooks Store is very much like the App Store or the iTunes Store. Books are categorised and searchable, and everything is charted so that you can see what is selling best.

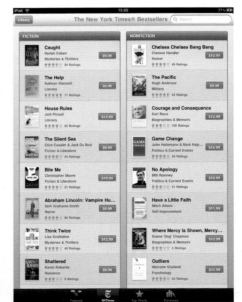

03 New York Times
There is even a section on the store where you can see the New York Times Bestseller list so you can pick and download titles from it. It provides a more objective listing than iBooks' own.

The iBooks Store homepage

Find your way around your new home for digital books

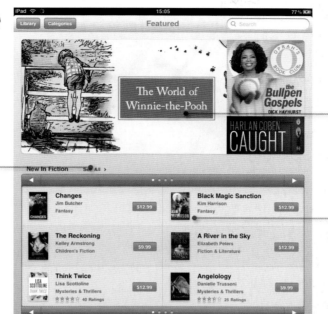

Promo perfection
Again, like the App Store, books are picked by Apple to be featured on the front of the Store. This positioning increases their sales no end, as you can imagine

See All
Use the See All button to get a bigger list from any given section. It's the same system that's used on the App Store

Easy Nav
Navigating through the Store with your fingers is easy. Tap buttons to see more and tap individual books to get more information

Tabs at the bottom
At the bottom of the interface there are four tabs, which will help you navigate through the Store and also see what you have already bought

Knowledge base
Be prepared
If you know that you are going to be without a data signal for any great period of time it's well worth downloading a couple of books so that you always have some reading material.

04 Free classics
Like the App Store, there are a huge number of free books. These tend to be the classics, so you can go ahead and get great content for nothing. Tap on the Free button and then tap Get Book.

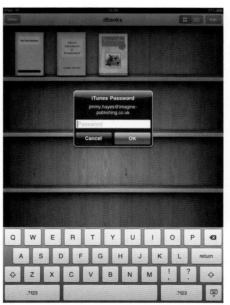

05 Password
You'll now be returned to the bookshelf and prompted to enter your iTunes account password. Do so and, once done, tap the OK button to begin the download.

06 New books
Your new books will now appear on the bookshelf and you'll see a progress bar as they download. Once downloaded, the book will become available to read at your leisure.

Getting started

Getting to know iBooks

Having an eBook reader on the iPad is very cool, so here's how to customise it to your liking…

Despite the conjecture, if you've actually used the iPad you'll know full well that it's much more than just a large iPod touch. The size really does make it feel like you're holding a full-blown computer in your hands, and no other app exemplifies the difference more than iBooks. When you're reading a book on the iPad it feels natural, it's easy to do, and we are certain that we'll be doing a lot more reading now that it's so simple to carry books around with us. The beauty of the iPad interface means that making changes to the way iBooks looks is very, very simple. Users can opt to make text bigger, change the font and alter the brightness of the book without having to leave the page they are reading. Try doing the same three operations on an iPhone and see how many times you have to leave and return to the page you are reading. iBooks is exceptional, so follow our quick tutorial on how to get more from the already excellent reading experience.

"Users can make text bigger, change the font and alter the brightness of the book"

True text
With the iPad being the size it is, reading is a complete joy. Once you have your fonts and the brightness set up how you like, you can read for hours on this device

Scrubber
You can also navigate through the app using the scrubber bar at the bottom of the page. Just drag your finger along the line

iBooks Font, size and brightness

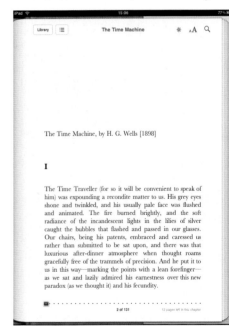

01 Open, bask
Open the iBooks app and then tap on the cover of a book on your shelf that you would like to read. The page is presented as if it were a real book but with options at the top and bottom.

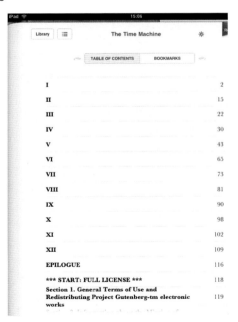

02 Contents
You can navigate from the contents page to a chapter simply by tapping on it and also, once you've been reading a while, you can head straight to your own bookmarks within the pages themselves.

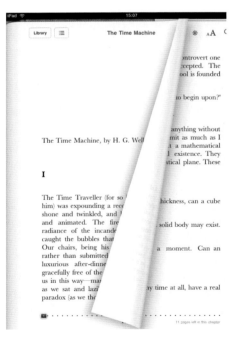

03 Curler
You can flip through pages by dragging from the right-hand side to the left, where you'll see the cool page curl. Or you can use the less cool but more functional tap on the right-hand side.

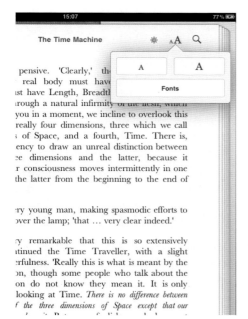

04 Font it

Tap on the 'aA' font button at the top of the page to access the menu where you can alter the book's font and text size. Tap the big A to increase font size and the smaller one to decrease it.

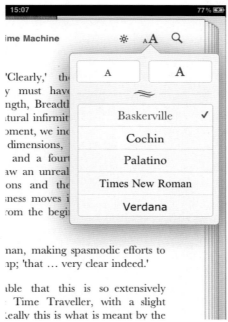

05 Font type

To change the font type, tap the Fonts button and then pick from the available options that are listed in the pop-out window. The selection should provide an alternative that suits you.

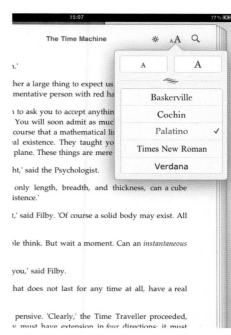

06 Tick it, watch it

Tap the font you wish to select and a tick will appear next to it. As with all the other changes you can make to the appearance of a book within iBooks, they happen instantly.

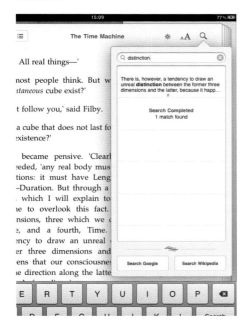

07 Spotlight index

Tap on the magnifying glass icon to bring up a search field. Every book on the iBook Store is fully indexed so you can instantly find individual words in a book. This will be really invaluable for textbooks.

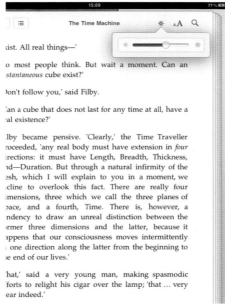

08 Brightness

Tap on the sunshine icon to bring up the brightness settings of the book. This only affects the levels within iBooks and doesn't translate to the rest of the iPad, so you won't have to change it back afterwards.

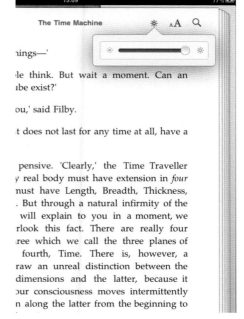

09 Suitable setting

Changing the brightness means that you can alter the reading light to whatever is most comfortable for your eyes. The brighter the ambient light, the brighter iBooks needs to be.

Getting started

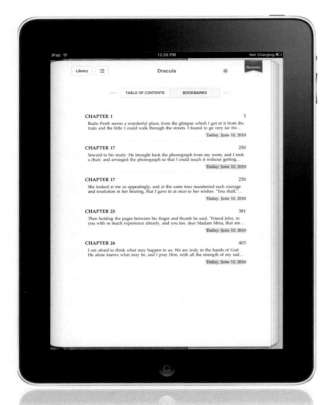

Creating Bookmarks in iBooks

Learn how to easily bookmark and highlight your favourite parts in digital books

I n the previous tutorials we have introduced you to the digital world of iBooks and all it has to offer you. iBooks is a fantastic eReader that allows you to carry a whole bookcase with you while on the move, customise the fonts, brightness and other settings to suit your needs and create a reading experience like no other. But having a wealth of books on your iPad could become hard to find your way around; thankfully, not only are your iBooks organised into a library that's easy to navigate, but you can also bookmark and highlight text so you can easily find the bit you are looking for among the piles and piles on your digital bookshelf.

The ability to highlight text is also a welcome feature. You can even select what colour you want to highlight the text in, which helps when you want to colour code certain bits to signify certain things. This is particularly useful for text book research. In this step-by-step tutorial we will show you how to easily use Bookmarks with iBooks.

"Easily find the bit you are looking for among the piles and piles on your digital bookshelf"

iBooks Using Bookmarks in iBooks

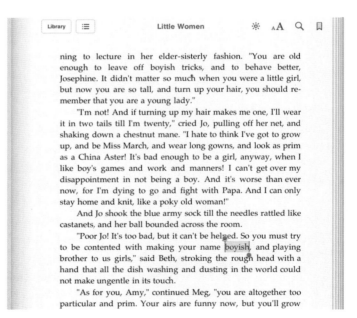

01 Select text to bookmark
Double tap anywhere (or press on a word) on the book to open the Options bar. Move the blue circles to select a region of text that you want to bookmark or highlight. It is similar to the cut-copy-paste mechanism available everywhere in the iOS.

02 Bookmark the selected text/region
Once the text has been selected, tap on the bookmark icon found in the top-right of the screen. Selecting the list icon next to the Library button will then take you to the bookmark menu. Tapping on the bookmark you want will take you to the relevant page.

iBooks Interface

Having a look inside iBooks

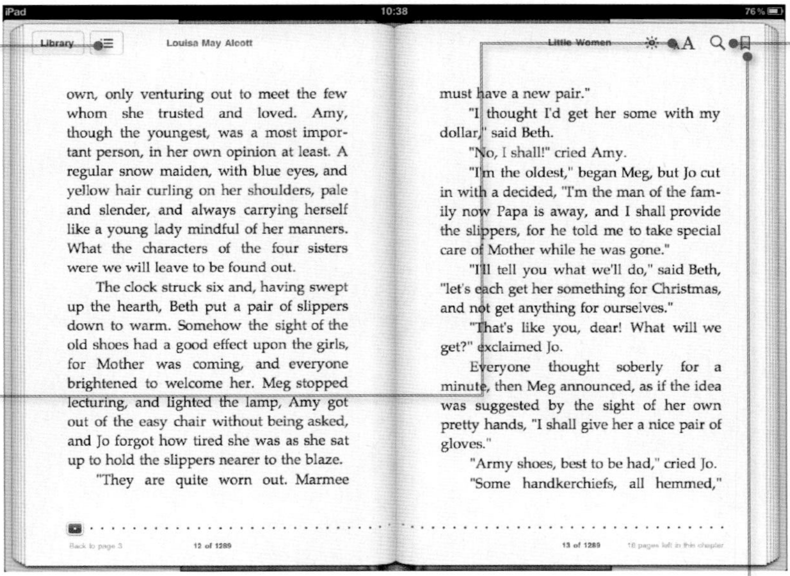
iPad
10:38
76%
Library
Louisa May Alcott
Little Women
own, only venturing out to meet the few whom she trusted and loved. Amy, though the youngest, was a most important person, in her own opinion at least. A regular snow maiden, with blue eyes, and yellow hair curling on her shoulders, pale and slender, and always carrying herself like a young lady mindful of her manners. What the characters of the four sisters were we will leave to be found out.
The clock struck six and, having swept up the hearth, Beth put a pair of slippers down to warm. Somehow the sight of the old shoes had a good effect upon the girls, for Mother was coming, and everyone brightened to welcome her. Meg stopped lecturing, and lighted the lamp, Amy got out of the easy chair without being asked, and Jo forgot how tired she was as she sat up to hold the slippers nearer to the blaze.
"They are quite worn out. Marmee
must have a new pair."
"I thought I'd get her some with my dollar," said Beth.
"No, I shall!" cried Amy.
"I'm the oldest," began Meg, but Jo cut in with a decided, "I'm the man of the family now Papa is away, and I shall provide the slippers, for he told me to take special care of Mother while he was gone."
"I'll tell you what we'll do," said Beth, "let's each get her something for Christmas, and not get anything for ourselves."
"That's like you, dear! What will we get?" exclaimed Jo.
Everyone thought soberly for a minute, then Meg announced, as if the idea was suggested by the sight of her own pretty hands, "I shall give her a nice pair of gloves."
"Army shoes, best to be had," cried Jo.
"Some handkerchiefs, all hemmed,"
12 of 1289
13 of 1289

Search book

Tapping this magnifying glass image allows you to do a full text search on the current book

TOC and Bookmarks

Tap on this button to access the Bookmarks and Table of Contents of the current book

Adjust font size

Tapping on this icon in the top right-hand corner allows you to adjust the font size

Bookmark

Tapping this icon allows you to instantly bookmark text

Knowledge base

EPUB file format

EPUB is an electronic book format that has become the industry standard developed by International Digital Publishing Forum (IDPF), allowing eBooks that use this format to be read on a wide variety of eReaders, from dedicated hardware to desktop software to online based readers. Files have the extension .epub. EPUB is designed for reflowable content, meaning that the text display can be optimised for the particular display device used by the reader of the EPUB-formatted book.

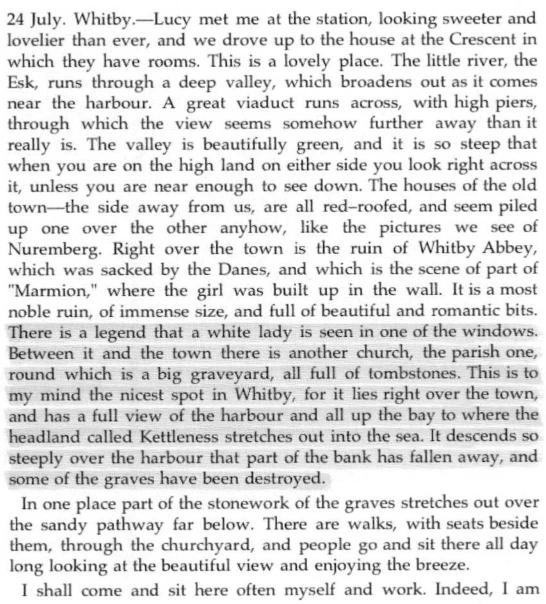
24 July. Whitby.—Lucy met me at the station, looking sweeter and lovelier than ever, and we drove up to the house at the Crescent in which they have rooms. This is a lovely place. The little river, the Esk, runs through a deep valley, which broadens out as it comes near the harbour. A great viaduct runs across, with high piers, through which the view seems somehow further away than it really is. The valley is beautifully green, and it is so steep that when you are on the high land on either side you look right across it, unless you are near enough to see down. The houses of the old town—the side away from us, are all red-roofed, and seem piled up one over the other anyhow, like the pictures we see of Nuremberg. Right over the town is the ruin of Whitby Abbey, which was sacked by the Danes, and which is the scene of part of "Marmion," where the girl was built up in the wall. It is a most noble ruin, of immense size, and full of beautiful and romantic bits. There is a legend that a white lady is seen in one of the windows. Between it and the town there is another church, the parish one, round which is a big graveyard, all full of tombstones. This is to my mind the nicest spot in Whitby, for it lies right over the town, and has a full view of the harbour and all up the bay to where the headland called Kettleness stretches out into the sea. It descends so steeply over the harbour that part of the bank has fallen away, and some of the graves have been destroyed.
In one place part of the stonework of the graves stretches out over the sandy pathway far below. There are walks, with seats beside them, through the churchyard, and people go and sit there all day long looking at the beautiful view and enjoying the breeze.
I shall come and sit here often myself and work. Indeed, I am

03 Highlight text

By simply pressing down on a single word or dragging over a block of text will bring up a menu. Then select Highlight.

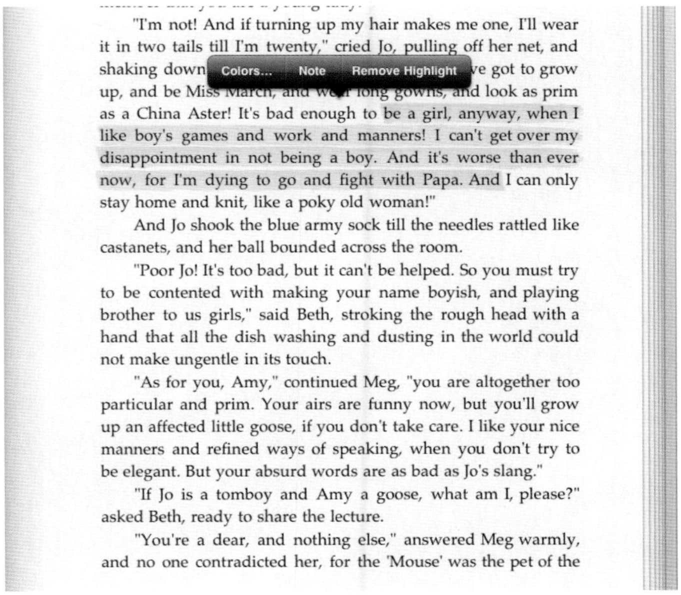
"I'm not! And if turning up my hair makes me one, I'll wear it in two tails till I'm twenty," cried Jo, pulling off her net, and shaking down
Colors... Note Remove Highlight
ve got to grow up, and be Miss March, and we... long gowns, and look as prim as a China Aster! It's bad enough to be a girl, anyway, when I like boy's games and work and manners! I can't get over my disappointment in not being a boy. And it's worse than ever now, for I'm dying to go and fight with Papa. And I can only stay home and knit, like a poky old woman!"
And Jo shook the blue army sock till the needles rattled like castanets, and her ball bounded across the room.
"Poor Jo! It's too bad, but it can't be helped. So you must try to be contented with making your name boyish, and playing brother to us girls," said Beth, stroking the rough head with a hand that all the dish washing and dusting in the world could not make ungentle in its touch.
"As for you, Amy," continued Meg, "you are altogether too particular and prim. Your airs are funny now, but you'll grow up an affected little goose, if you don't take care. I like your nice manners and refined ways of speaking, when you don't try to be elegant. But your absurd words are as bad as Jo's slang."
"If Jo is a tomboy and Amy a goose, what am I, please?" asked Beth, ready to share the lecture.
"You're a dear, and nothing else," answered Meg warmly, and no one contradicted her, for the 'Mouse' was the pet of the

04 Change colour of bookmarked/highlighted text

You can change the colour of bookmarked text to organise it better. You can choose from five colours, namely yellow, green, blue, pink and purple. To change the colour, tap on the highlighted text, tap the Colors… option and then select a different colour.

The next step

> **"Keynote lets you create presentations wherever you are without the binding need for wires"**

Get to grips with the iPad's more in-depth features with our handy guides

106 Get to grips with Pages
Word processing is now available while on the move

108 Create spreadsheets with Numbers
Number-crunching comes to the iPad

110 Perform your presentations in style with Keynote
Build a presentation away from your desktop

112 Use Dropbox to transfer files
Utilise cloud-based file transfers

114 Using the Voice Memos for iPad app
Record sound with this free application

116 Stream content with AirPlay
Send audio, television, film and music to other devices

118 Print from your iPad with AirPrint
Send iPad documents straight to a printer

120 Stream video directly to your iPad with Air Video
Watch video content straight from your Mac on your iPad

122 Get things done using Taska
Make a to-do list and organise tasks

124 Download and read eBooks using Kindle
An alternative to iBooks for digital reading

126 Make your voice heard using Twitter
Tweet to your heart's content on the iPad

128 Using the Facebook app
Keep social while on the move

Tip one
Presentations via iPad

Tip two
Stream with AirPlay

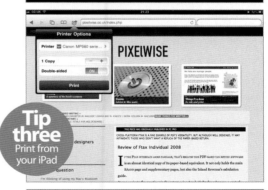

Tip three
Print from your iPad

Tip four
Twitter made simple

Get to grips with Pages

Apple's Pages takes the mobile word processing experience to a whole new level

Pages is not like most word processors – it combines the most used features in an interface which includes very few icons. Getting to know the app is not difficult, but it helps to understand where the main functions reside to get you started, and doing so will open up the power within. Despite the sparse interface it is packed with formatting options and clever tricks that make previously tiresome manoeuvres a thing of the past. For example, you can move an embedded image around an article and the words will automatically reposition themselves around it, and the included templates are completely customisable, which enables you to get creating in no time at all.

Not all specific needs are catered for, such as a word count, but Apple has done a good job of defining the most used functions that people need and being able to share your creations without touching a desktop is another advantage. You can even decide which format to save these documents in. In this guide we will be showing you how to get started with Pages. As we stated earlier, this is not a standard word processor, but it may well become the one you use more than any other.

Pages   Create stunning documents on the move

01 Grab the app

Search for 'Pages' in iTunes and purchase and install as normal. £5.99 may seem expensive for an iTunes app, but it is in fact very good value for a word processor with so many features.

02 Have a look around

Pages is so obviously visual in the way it is designed that you could just have a wander around the icons and start typing, but the best place to start is the pre-loaded user manual.

03 Create your first document

In the first screen tap the '+' icon at the bottom and then tap New document. This will bring up a screen with templates on. You can choose anything from a blank page to a party invite.

Making the most of Pages

Learn all the tricks of the Pages trade…

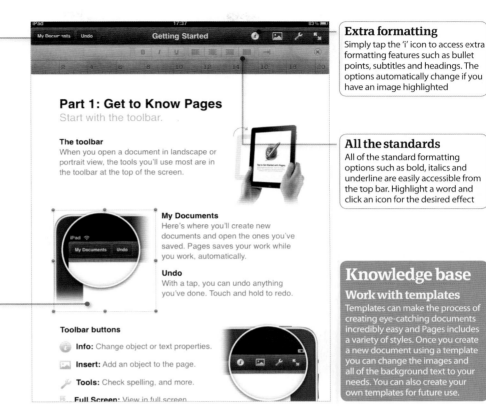

Part 1: Get to Know Pages
Start with the toolbar.

The toolbar
When you open a document in landscape or portrait view, the tools you'll use most are in the toolbar at the top of the screen.

My Documents
Here's where you'll create new documents and open the ones you've saved. Pages saves your work while you work, automatically.

Undo
With a tap, you can undo anything you've done. Touch and hold to redo.

Toolbar buttons

Info: Change object or text properties.

Insert: Add an object to the page.

Tools: Check spelling, and more.

Full Screen: View in full screen.

Document handling
Your completed documents are never far away. A tap of the 'My Documents' icon will bring up a page showing all of your saved work. Each document is saved automatically after every change

Easy image manipulation
Once inserted, images can be resized, moved and even twisted to the position you need. The words will automatically move to around them and into the right position

Extra formatting
Simply tap the 'i' icon to access extra formatting features such as bullet points, subtitles and headings. The options automatically change if you have an image highlighted

All the standards
All of the standard formatting options such as bold, italics and underline are easily accessible from the top bar. Highlight a word and click an icon for the desired effect

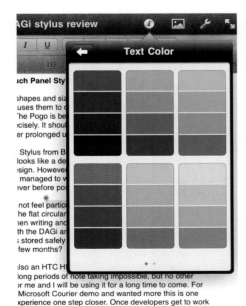

04 Test the options
Type a few words and then check the formatting options at the top. Select words by tapping and holding, at which point you can use the icons to format the text. Clicking 'i' gives further options.

05 Delve deeper
Other options include a document setup wizard, defined by the top-right spanner icon and a quick tap of the picture icon lets you insert an image into your document.

06 Share your work
You never need to save your work because Pages does it whenever a change is made, but you can export it to PDF, Pages or Word format and send by email with the tap of one icon.

Create spreadsheets with Numbers

Use Numbers to create serious or silly spreadsheets to suit all tastes

Spreadsheets are a part of everyone's lives these days and have taken on multiple roles in business and at home. Most spreadsheet programs tend to focus on the business side because this is where they are mainly used, but spreadsheets have a myriad of other uses that aren't often explored.

Numbers puts multiple uses front and centre with special templates built in and also brings a new way of working to the mobile user. However, the interface and function locations may feel alien to those that have used Excel for a long time and so a short introduction will help you to get to grips with the app quickly. There are a lot of functions built in to Numbers and some of these are not obvious, so take a look at these simple steps to start number-crunching straight away.

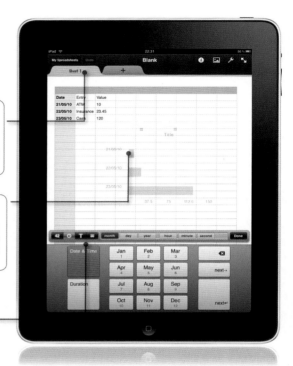

Tabs, tabs, tabs
You can create as many linked tabs as you like by simply tapping the '+' icon. When you need to view them, just move your finger from left to right until you find the one you need

Touchy feely
You can adjust and select single cells, rows and columns with your finger and even though it feels strange at first, you will soon wonder how you ever created spreadsheets with just a mouse

Four icons
These four small icons are the shop window to a huge array of advanced functions including specialised calculations and standard formats

Numbers Explore the power of this spreadsheet app

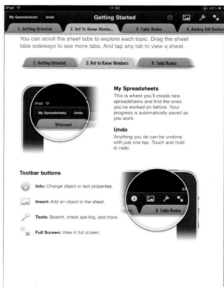

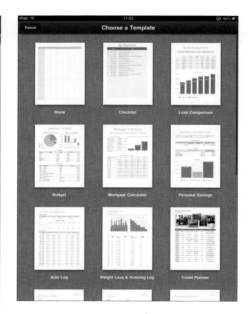

01 Grab the app
As with all iPad apps, Numbers is available from the iTunes App Store. It costs £5.99, and although this may seem steep, it is excellent value even if you only need spreadsheets occasionally. Once you have installed it you are ready to start.

02 Check out the manual
Apple has included a manual in Numbers which highlights the various solutions it can be used for. Because of the large number of features on offer it is recommended that you spare a few minutes to read every page – this will speed things up later on.

03 Your first spreadsheet
Tap the '+' icon at the bottom and then click the New Spreadsheet option. You will now be offered a choice of templates which includes everything from a blank sheet to a mortgage calculator – there's everything you could ever need.

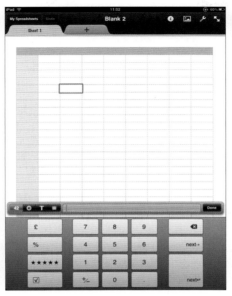

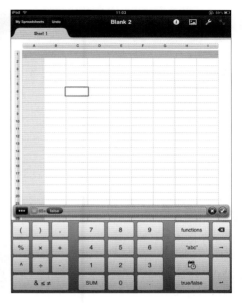

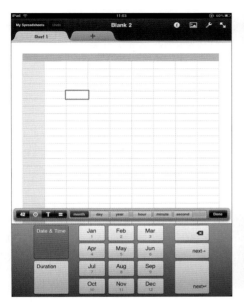

04 Adding data

Choose the blank template option in the top-left corner and double-tap an empty cell anywhere in the sheet. This brings up a dialog with four icons for numbers, date/time, text and formulas. Choose the one you wish to use.

05 Handy shortcuts

Tapping any of the four icons will bring up a dialog with shortcuts pertinent to the data you want to input. For example the number icon will bring up a number pad plus a percentage button and even a star rating function and tick box.

06 Use the data

Once you have understood where each function resides you can now do something with your content. If you tap the '=' icon you can choose from a wide range of simple functions that will pop up such as 'SUM' and true/false.

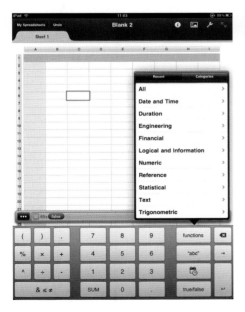

07 Advanced functions

The functions button is a window to some serious capability and includes categories of advanced functions such as Trigonometric, Engineering and Statistical. It is fair to say that almost everyone is catered for by Numbers.

08 Add some media

Once you have your basic data built you can then tap the picture icon in the top-right and insert photos, tables and shapes which will help to make the data more visual. There are six pages of shapes and also six pages of table styles.

09 Practise your touch

Numbers is touch only and this will present problems at first, but the more you practise the more natural it begins to feel. The interface looks simple, but it hides a huge range of options that will become second nature with time.

The next step

Perform your presentations in style with Keynote

Keynote for iPad brings the Apple ethos of keeping things simple to the world of presentations

Creating presentations in PowerPoint has caused as much scratching of heads over the years as almost any other software solution. Despite this it has been widely used in the corporate world and to this day dominates the presentation software market. Keynote for iPad brings with it the advantages of not only being mobile, but is also incredibly easy to use.

Because the iPad is finger driven, Apple has had to do away with the preciseness this type of software normally requires and has managed to make the entire process finger friendly and much quicker than the competition. It will still take some time to get used to, though, because the commands are different and at times it feels almost too easy. In this guide we will show you how to create your first presentation and how to make the most of the features and the fact that you can create wherever you are without the need for wires.

What a nice place to live. Bit quiet though...

"Apple has managed to make the entire presentation process finger friendly and much quicker"

Using Keynote

Make your presentations look professional without needing to touch your desktop PC or Mac

Check your slides
All of your slides are available in the left-hand column and are previewed in great detail. You can also drag and drop them to change the order in which they will appear

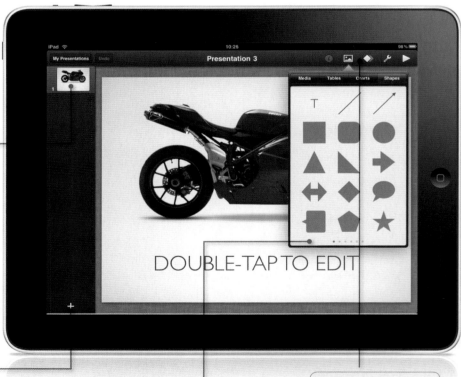

DOUBLE-TAP TO EDIT

New slides
Adding a new slide requires a single tap on the '+' icon. Almost every function in Keynote only requires a tap or two and is highly intuitive to use

Shapes, text and more
The media available is almost unlimited and everything from simple text to photos and charts are available to you. You can then manipulate them once inserted into a slide

Use the icons
These four simple icons hold within them a wealth of tweaks and tricks that will help you build a presentation in no time at all

Keynote Build a Keynote presentation

01 Get Keynote
Keynote is available on the iTunes App Store for £5.99 and is part of the iWork for iPad solution. All you need to do is purchase it and install it on your iPad as normal.

02 Read the manual
As you would expect from Apple, a manual is included in the app which is designed to get you up and running quickly.

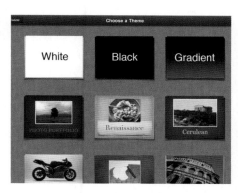

03 Create your first presentation
Click the '+' icon at the bottom and then select New Presentation. You can choose from 12 themes, but for the purposes of this guide select the White one.

04 Build your first slide
On the first slide, double-tap the photo and tap the small icon that pops up. You can replace the photo with an image of your choice from the photo library.

05 Use your words
Double-tap the text and add your own words. When done, tap on the words and tap the 'i' icon. This will bring up a selection of styles and colours for the text.

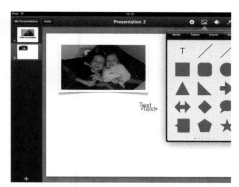

06 The important second slide
Tap the '+' icon on the bottom-left to create a second slide. Tap the picture icon at the top and then choose the 'Charts' tab. Tap the 'T' to insert a new text box.

07 Add media
You will have noticed from the previous step that you can insert photos, tables, charts and many different shapes through the one command.

08 Time for tweaks
You can manipulate your media easily within Keynote. Tap a photo and then hold two fingers on it – you can now spin it round to any angle you like.

09 Share your work
Once you've finished you can share your work by tapping the left icon in the main document view. This will let you send it via email or to iWork.com.

Use Dropbox to transfer files

Want to transfer many files between your Mac, iPhone and iPad? Learn how life can be so much easier with a free service called Dropbox. You'll never need a USB stick again…

With cloud computing on the increase, life is getting easier and more convenient for all computer users. Take Dropbox for example; until recently the only way to transfer files between two computers was to either email them or copy them onto a USB stick. A tiresome chore if you regularly work using several machines. Thankfully, Dropbox makes this task so much easier. By installing the app on your Mac, PC, iPhone or iPad, any files you drop onto it will be accessible – instantly – on all the other devices. No longer will you need to carry a USB stick in your pocket or search through the drawers for one, as everything you need will be on one of your favourite devices.

Best of all, a 2GB account is free! Follow us over the next two pages as we explain how to set up and use Dropbox to copy files between your Mac and iPad. It's so easy and convenient you'll wonder how you ever managed without it…

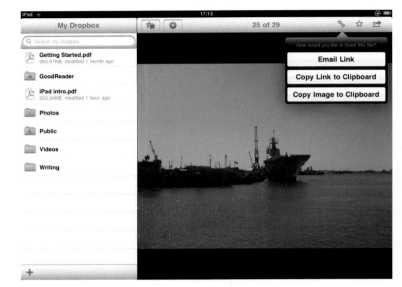

"No longer will you need to carry a USB stick in your pocket to transfer files"

Using Dropbox on the iPad
Find your way around this file transfer service

Space Used
Dropbox includes 2GB of free online storage (you can purchase more from the website). To see how much space you've used, tap the Settings button

Camera settings
Select the quality of photos uploaded from your iPad by pressing the Camera button – a slider enables you to tweak the image quality. Note that higher settings will take longer to upload, and take up more space

Navigation
Use the menu on the left to browse your files and folders. When viewing a file, you can pinch-to-zoom, scroll and click-and-hold to navigate and share files

Passcode Lock
Prevent others from accessing your Dropbox account by setting a Passcode Lock – it works exactly the same as the passcode built into the iPhone OS. Just remember the code you use!

Dropbox Transfer files through the cloud

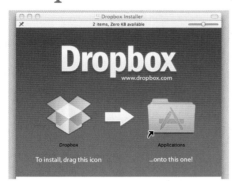

01 Download and sign up

Install Dropbox on every device that you wish to share files between. It's free from the App Store and **www.dropbox.com**.

02 Start on the Mac

If installed on a Mac you'll see a Dropbox folder under the Places tab on every Finder window. Drag any files you wish to transfer into this folder.

03 In the cloud

These files are automatically copied to the Dropbox server in the cloud, and you can now access them from your iPad. Load up Dropbox and sign in.

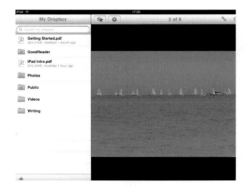

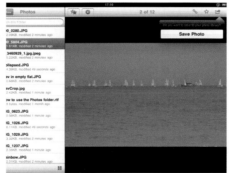

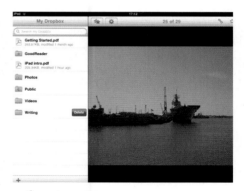

04 Browsing files

Turn your iPad on its side to go into landscape mode and you'll see a menu down the left-hand side – here's where you can browse folders.

05 Saving photos

As you can see, we've copied some photos to our Dropbox Photos folder. To save a photo to your iPad, press the share button in the top-right corner.

06 Delete files

You can delete files and folders by swiping a finger across them. These files will be deleted from your Dropbox account – not just your iPad.

07 Share files

You can share files with friends by emailing them a weblink of the file in your account. Tap the chain link in the top-right corner, and enter an email address.

08 Upload photos

To upload files from your iPad to your account, tap the + button in the bottom-left corner. You can upload photos from your Photo Album.

09 Another app

To open a file in the relevant app (for example a .pages file in Pages), tap the share button in the top-right corner and select the app.

Using the Voice Memos for iPad app

There's no native Voice Memos app on the iPad, so use this great free option instead…

W hile we're absolutely sure that the iPad App Store will throw out any number of novel uses for a 10-inch touch screen, we were a little surprised that Apple didn't include the voice recording app from the iPhone 3GS on this device. We could pontificate over the reasons, but it's all academic as there is an incredibly Apple-esque app out there which is free to download. This app is beautifully made, it looks great on the screen and it works incredibly well. The free version limits a couple of features, like emailing the memo, but for the purpose of recording thoughts and the like it's more than adequate. The menu system is as simple and Apple-esque as you would like, and within a few minutes of discovery you can know everything there is to know. It's extra functionality like this that elevates Apple devices beyond the combination of great hardware and in-house software. It's a very useful app that once you get used to will become a go-to application when you don't have time to type or just want to hear how something sounds.

> "This app is beautifully made, looks great and works incredibly well"

Voice Memos Record and tag a voice memo

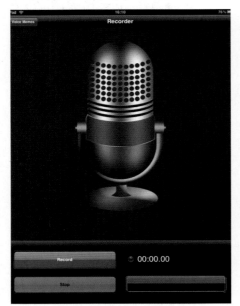

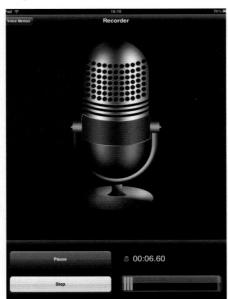

01 Load it, record it
Install and load the Voice Memos for iPad app and then hit the large red Record button to begin recording. The iPad microphone lives at the bottom of the device below the home button.

02 Level check
The green bars at the bottom of the interface indicate when the microphone detects audio. Make sure the level doesn't run into the red, otherwise the sound will distort.

03 Finished and view
When you've finished recording you can view the stored memos by tapping the Voice Memos button to reveal the drop-down menu. Memos are organised by date.

Record voice memos on the iPad

Download the free Voice Memos app and get recording

Knowledge base

Sound

The microphone on the iPad isn't of amazing quality, but it is certainly good enough for basic use. The speakers on the iPad are of much better quality, and resemble those of a MacBook more than the iPhone.

04 Playback

Tap on the blue arrow button to play the voice memo. You can see the progress as the memo plays. You can also see how long is left and how much has been played.

05 Add a tag

It is possible to add a tag to each memo so you can get a clearer idea what each one is. Tap on the blue arrow in the top-right of the pop-out window to see the next screen.

06 Tick it

On this screen you can tick the tag you want to label the memo with (Podcast, Interview, Lecture, etc). If you want you can also create a customised, more specific tag.

The next step

Stream content with AirPlay

You can turn your iPad into your home media hub that all the family can share by streaming audio and video to other devices in your house. Here's how…

While it's great to be able to carry your favourite films, photos and music with you on your iPad, let's be honest: the joy is a personal one, as the iPad's speakers and screen are hardly built for sharing with a wider audience.

Or at least it would be without the iPad's killer feature: AirPlay. It allows you to stream your iPad's music, video and images wirelessly across a local network.

The only extra you need to use AirPlay is a compatible device to stream your iPad's content to. This could be an AppleTV, AirPlay-enabled stereo speakers – of which there are several on the market – or an AirPort Express wireless base station, which comes with a socket that enables it to connect to a home stereo system. A button tap is all it takes to free your audio and video and watch films on the big screen, or listen to your music collection on your best speakers. No wires required.

"A tap is all it takes to free your audio and video and watch films on a big screen"

AirPlay Set up your AirPlay connection

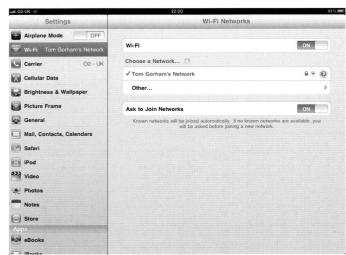

01 Check wireless settings

AirPlay works over a local Wi-Fi network, so check that your iPad and the device you're streaming to are on the same network. You can set this up on the iPad by tapping Settings and choosing the Wi-Fi option. If your network is secured, you will need to enter its password.

02 Open the media

When your devices are properly connected, start playing the media on the iPad that you want to stream to another device. When you play a movie or a song on your iPad tap the AirPlay icon (a hollow rectangle with a solid triangle) that appears on the media controller.

AirPlay on the iPad in action

AirPlay is an impressive technology, but it's pretty simple to use

More than video

It isn't just the media itself that can be sent over AirPlay. Song titles, artists, album names and artwork can all appear on AirPlay-enabled speakers that have graphical displays

AirPlay's icon

The AirPlay icon itself is just a simple box with an arrow. The same icon appears on all iOS devices, and in iTunes on the Mac and PC too

More than video

It isn't just the media itself that can be sent over AirPlay. Song titles, artists, album names and artwork can all appear on AirPlay-enabled speakers that have graphical displays

Audio or video?

The speaker icon here indicates that only audio will be streamed to the external device. If you see a TV icon instead, video will also be streamed over AirPlay

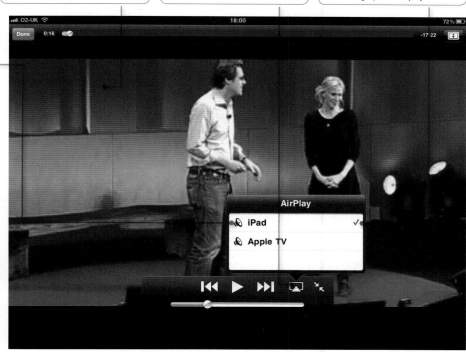

Knowledge base

AirPlay everywhere

AirPlay is a clever wireless technology the usefulness of which isn't restricted to the iPad. In fact, any iOS device with iOS 4.2 or later installed on it can use AirPlay – and so can the iTunes application on Mac OSX. AirPlay features are also present in Apple's free Remote iPad and iPhone app, which allows you to control an iTunes library from an iOS device. But not all video can be streamed using AirPlay. At the time of writing, video streaming from the iPad is limited to media streamed from Apple's own apps – other apps can only stream audio.

03 Choose your output

When you tap the AirPlay icon, a pop-up menu will appear, offering a choice of AirPlay-enabled devices. The currently selected output has a tick next to it, and it should be your iPad. Tap the name of the device you want to stream to.

04 Streaming in action

Unfortunately, you're not able to watch the same video in two places at once. Once you have selected another output device from the list, the video or audio is sent there within a couple of seconds. The iPad's screen will go blank!

The next step

Print from your iPad with AirPrint

Yes, believe it or not, you can actually print from your iPad – but there are some tricks you should know about. Here are our secrets to iPad printing…

When critics sought to find flaws in the iPad on its release last year, one weakness they focused on was its inability to print. At the time, for a permanent record of anything on your iPad's screen you had to email a copy to your Mac or PC and print it from there.

But the arrival of iOS 4.2 ended those complaints by bringing printing to the iPad's set of features. And in true Apple fashion it's a cinch to use – even if it does have limitations.

AirPrint works with most popular iPad applications, such as Pages, Safari and Photos. It works over a local Wi-Fi network, so to use it you need to be on the same network as the printer you plan to use. The catch is that the iPad only prints to AirPrint-compatible printers, currently restricted to a limited range (a full list can be found at **http://bit.ly/euwjbk**). But the good news is that some third-party utilities enable you to print to any printer on your network.

"AirPrint works with most popular iPad applications, such as Pages and Safari"

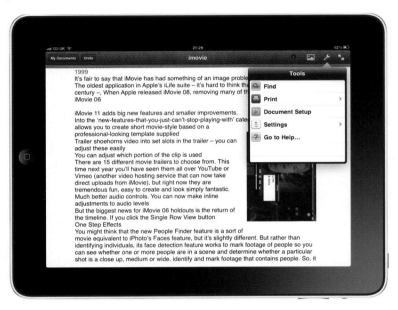

AirPrint How to print a webpage

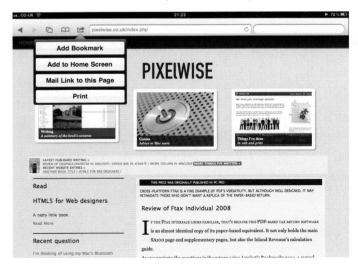

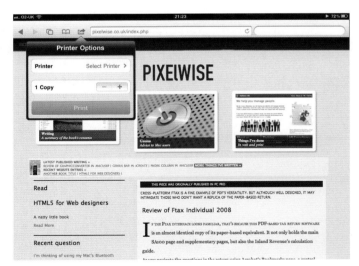

01 Choose the page to print
Many iPad apps now support printing, and most use the same technique. To print a page in Safari, for example, navigate to the page you want to print, click the arrow icon at the top of the screen, and select the Print option from the drop-down menu.

02 Choose the printer
Your iPad doesn't automatically know which printer you want to print to. The first time you print from an application, you will be prompted to select a printer. You will have to tap Select Printer to make your choice from the available printers.

Printing on the iPad

Most iPad apps follow the same approach when printing

Find the Print icon
In most apps that support printing, the printing option is found under the same 'arrow in box' icon

Options
Currently Apple restricts the type of printer you can print to, but here we're using the Printopia utility to print to a non-AirPrint-compatible Canon printer

Switching printers
The iPad remembers your chosen printer, but if you want to change printer, just tap the printer in the list and you will be taken to another drop-down menu showing all available options

Number of copies
Quickly choose the number of copies you would like to print by tapping the '+' or '-' buttons. Depending on the options that your printer supports, you may see additional choices here

Knowledge base
Print to any printer
So what do you do if you don't have a AirPrint-ready printer? One way around this limitation is to use Printopia (**www.ecamm.com/mac/printopia**), a Mac utility that when installed lets your iPad print to any printer attached to your Mac, even it isn't AirPrint compatible. It also adds a 'virtual printer' that lets you send PDFs or JPEGs directly from your iPad to your Mac.

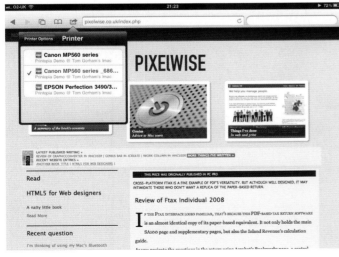

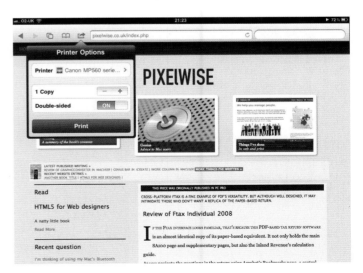

03 The printer list
As long as you're on the same Wi-Fi network as your printers, you should see every AirPrint-enabled device in this list. Choose the device that you would like to print the webpage to, so you can select any further printing options.

04 Choosing options
Depending on the printer you have selected, you may get other printing options. For example, if your printer supports double-sided printing, this may appear as an option. When you're happy with the options you have chosen, tap the 'Print' button and the page will be printed.

The next step

Stream video directly to your iPad with Air Video

Discover how to stream video from your Mac to your iPad. It's easy, free, and saves you time

With its large 9.7" Multi-Touch display, the iPad is perfect for watching video content away from your Mac and TV. Getting video onto it is another matter however. iTunes is great at converting QuickTime videos or syncing content from iTunes, but if you have any video content that's not in a native Mac format (such as .avi/.wmv/.mkv) then you're looking at a time consuming and expensive endeavour to convert it.

Thankfully, Air Video is here to help. It streams any video to your iPad from your Mac – and we mean any video. Whatever video content you have, Air Video will play it, even native Windows video files and xvids. It's incredibly easy to set-up and use, and costs only £1.79. There's even a free version for you to try in the App Store.

Follow us over the next two pages as we explain how it works, plus we offer some very handy tips for getting the best picture quality. So what are you waiting for? Let's get going!

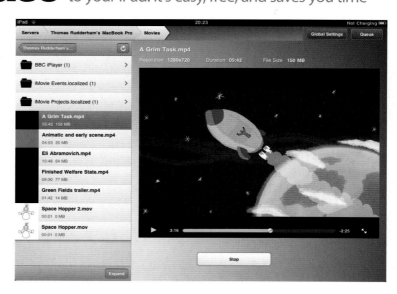

"Whatever video content you have, Air Video will play it, and it's easy to use"

Use Air Video to stream your videos

Stream directly from your Mac to your iPad

Queue content
The Queue button in the top-right corner of the screen will display any videos that are currently rendering on your Mac for later playback. You can stop any videos and edit the queue order from this window too

Multiple locations
You can share any number of folders on your Mac. Simply add them using Air Video Server and they will be accessible on your iPad

Subtitles
If the video has built-in subtitles or separate audio tracks, then you can enable or swap between these by tapping the buttons above the window

Higher quality
To save rendering time and achieve a slightly higher-quality picture, tap the Convert button. Your Mac will now render the chosen video for you to watch at a later date – without instant playback

Air Video Stream video wirelessly

01 Get downloading
Download Air Video to your iPad from the App Store, plus Air Video Server for your Mac from **www. inmethod.com**. Now open the Air Video Server.

02 Choose a location
Click the Add Disk Folder button at the bottom of the screen, and choose whichever folder contains the videos you wish to watch on your iPad.

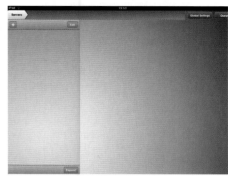

03 Load up your iPad
Your Mac is now running a video server that your iPad can connect to. Open Air Video on your iPad and click the plus icon in the top-left corner.

04 Local network
You'll see your Mac listed in the field to the left of the screen. Simply tap it to add it to your Server list. Now tap on your Mac again to access your videos.

05 Videos listed
You'll see every video listed on your Mac, each with a preview thumbnail. When you tap a video, the main window will display a number of options.

06 Playing video
Tap on the 'Play With Live Conversion' button to immediately play the video. Depending on the speed of your Mac this may take a few seconds.

07 Controls
Air Video plays content exactly the same as any movie on your iPad, so you can scrub through the video and play it full-screen using standard controls.

08 Other options
To convert a video for later playback, simply tap the Convert button and Air Video will render the video in the background. You can also send it to iTunes.

09 Video resolution
Tap the Global Setting button to change the resolution. You can max the settings for crystal clear video, but your Mac will take longer to stream video.

Get things done using Taska

Don't let your chores get you down. This fabulous app will help you break tasks down into categorised to-do lists, to help you get things done!

Sometimes work deadlines and household chores can pile up so high that we don't know where to begin, leaving us unable to deal with our workload. Relatively simple tasks like posting a parcel might keep popping into our heads, only to be brushed away as we feel too busy to deal with them at the moment. This means that we can spend more time worrying about certain jobs than it would take to do actually do them.

Fortunately this well-designed app will help you break up multiple tasks up into manageable to-do lists, so that you can make progress in a more organised (and less stressful) fashion.

We'll show you how to use Taska to create a simple to-do list. After adding tasks you'll be able to tick them off as your complete them. You can build on the skills you'll learn to create lists for any kind of project, whether it's work-based or a simple shopping list. We'll also show you how to assign icons to lists to help categorise them. Prepare to get things done!

> ## "Break up tasks up into manageable to-do lists, so you can make progress"

Taska Create a to-do list

01 Create a list

Launch the Taska app and click on the yellow List tab. Click on the + icon at the top left of the screen. A New List window will appear. Name the list to help you identify it. Choose an icon like the clipboard checklist. Click Save to create your list.

02 Add a task

The new list's icon appears in the left column. To add items to the list click on the + icon at the top right. Click on Task. Label the task. Tap Due Date and give yourself a deadline. Set a specific time by tapping in the All Day field. Leave a note if required.

Take things to Taska

Get things done more efficiently with these top Taska tools

Action stations
Files that have been dragged to the Action icon are colour coded yellow to draw attention to them. They'll still appear in the list that they were originally created in

Order your lists
You can change the way Taska presents the items on your list. Click here to list things to do by priority. Alternatively you can list items according to their due date

Drag and drop
Re-organise the contents of any list by clicking on a task and then dragging it to a different icon. Set up as many lists as you like do deal with the different areas in your life

Ticked off
Simply tick this box when a job gets done. Initially the task will become greyed out. When you return to Taska later you'll find the task has been moved to the Completed box

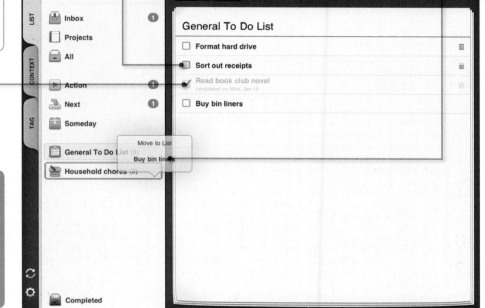

Knowledge base

Take action

When setting up a task you can give it a due date, but there's a risk that the deadline day will come without you taking action. To help you deal with the task more effectively click on Due Date. Set a due date and then click the Add to Action tab. You can now use the scroll wheel to make Taska add the item to the Action category a few days before the due date. This will add a yellow Action icon to the task at the appropriate time, enabling you to see which tasks require action.

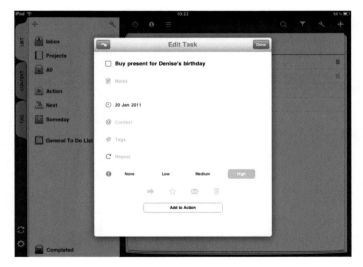

03 Prioritise task

Click Save to add the task to the list. Add other tasks in the same way. To prioritise a task click on it to open the Edit Task window. Choose from Low, Medium or High. Click Done. The task will have one, two or three red bars by it depending on the urgency.

04 Job done!

Prioritise really urgent tasks by dragging them to the Next icon. Or you can pop them in your Inbox. Once a task has been completed simply tick the box to its left. Completed tasks will disappear from the list (but you can still see them in the Completed box).

The next step

Download and read eBooks using Kindle

Build up a library of books on your iPad's Kindle app, so you can read your favourite authors on the go

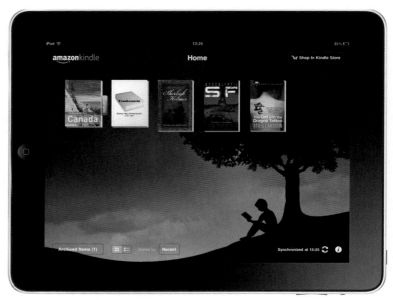

Before iPads where invented, we had to lug our holiday reading around on slabs of processed dead tree. Printed books (especially chunky hard backs with massive page counts) took up valuable space in our suitcase, and ate into our precious baggage weight allowance to boot.

In these digital days, the Kindle app provides a much more convenient way of storing our holiday (or day to day) reading. As well as enabling us to read electronic books (or eBooks) on the iPad's screen, we can use Kindle to shop for them as well. This saves us the hassle of popping out to the high street bookshop (or having to anxiously wait for the postman to deliver books in time for our holiday's departure date).

Kindle was initially a handheld tablet invented by retail giant Amazon to enable book lovers to read digital copies of books. However, iPad owners can download the free Kindle app and turn their iPad into a Kindle reader with ease (saving them the expense of buying a dedicated digital book reader).

"In these digital days, the Kindle app for iPad provides a much more convenient way of storing our reading"

Kindle Learn how to get eBooks onto your iPad

01 Open Kindle

Download the Kindle app for free from the App Store and install it on your iPad. Tapping on the Kindle icon takes you to the Home screen. This is where your books will be stored. To find some reading material, click on the 'Shop in Kindle Store' button at the top right.

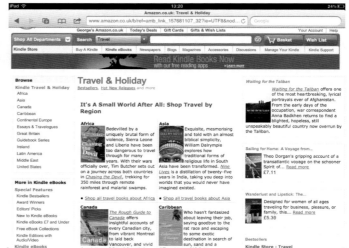

02 Go shopping

The Kindle eBook store is part of the Amazon website, so there are plenty of books to choose from. Peruse one of the featured new books on the Kindle Store's homepage, or browse through your favourite categories by clicking on a link like Travel & Holiday.

Interact with a Kindle eBook

Discover the extra bells and whistles you get from an eBook

Interactive links
As with webpages, links to content in other parts of the eBook are underlined, so you can jump to different chapters or sections of the book in a click. This interactivity gives eBooks the edge over their paper predecessors

Explore bookmarks
Click here to jump to specific notes or bookmarks that you've created. This saves you the hassle of trying to remember where important information is stored in your eBook

Customise pages
Lost your glasses? No problem! Use this section to create your own big print edition in a click, or inverse the text so that you're reading white letters on a black background

Notes and highlight
To help you find a particular bit of text at a later date, hold your finger down on it and drag to make a selection. You can then type in a note or select a highlight colour

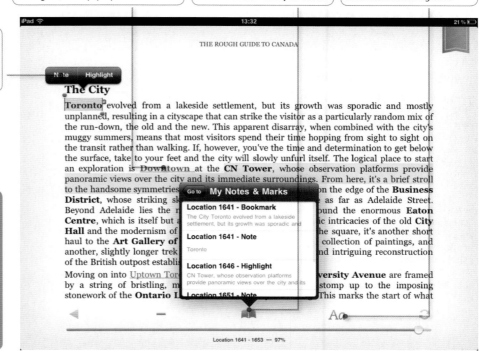

Knowledge base

Fabulous freebies

As well as downloading sample chapters from many new eBooks, you can download entire books for free using the Kindle eBook reader. This is a great way to catch up with the classics of literature. Simply click on the link to the online Kindle store to launch it in Safari, then scroll down to the Free eBook Editions link in the Special Features section. You can then browse through thousands of books in Kindle's Popular Classics range and enjoy adventure tales featuring Conan Doyle's Sherlock Holmes, or chill your spine with the work of HP Lovecraft.

03 Download your book

Tap on a thumbnail to discover more about a particular book, and read customer reviews to help you make an informed choice. If you fancy buying the book tap the 'Buy now with 1-click' button. Alternatively, download a free sample chapter. Make sure you set the 'Deliver to the iPad' option.

04 Start reading

To read a downloaded book, tap on its cover in your Kindle Home screen. Turn pages by tapping the screen (or swiping left or right). You can tap the top-right corner to bookmark a page (instead of creasing down the corner in traditional printed book).

The next step

Make your voice heard using Twitter

Follow the day-to-day activities of your favourite folk and share the latest news from your own life with this super social networking app

A s you'll probably know by now, Twitter enables you to share short messages (no more than 144 characters in length) with the rest of the world – much like the status updates in Facebook. Even if you don't have a Twitter account it's impossible to avoid the influence of this social networking site. Politicians, banks and your favourite TV personality are more likely to have a Twitter account than not, so they can update you on their latest activities.

The iPad Twitter app enables you to subscribe to – or follow – the Twitter broadcasts of particular people. You can also broadcast – or tweet – your own thoughts, and you may pick up some followers along the way who will hang off your every word.

To follow this tutorial you'll need to install the free Twitter app from the iTunes Store. Once you launch the app you can click Sign Up to create your own Twitter account, or Sign In if you've already got one. We'll then show you how make your own tweets and find interesting people to follow.

> "Even if you don't have a Twitter account it's impossible to avoid the influence of this site"

Twitter Start tweeting with this app

01 Set up a profile

To help future followers know who you are, click Profile, then Edit Profile. Click Profile Image to find a mug shot from your iPad's Photo Library – you'll need to use a small photo as Twitter doesn't like large files. Tap bio and write a brief description of yourself then click Save.

02 Make a tweet

To tweet, tap the icon at the screen's bottom left. Type into the New Tweet window. As you're limited to a message containing 144 characters, you'll see a countdown at the bottom left of the Tweet window. You can even attach a photo to the tweet. Click Send when you're ready.

Twitter in action

Get to know your way around the Twitter interface

Timeline
When any of the people that you follow make a tweet, it will appear in this scrolling Timeline page. To find out more about a particular person simply click on their photo and their profile page will appear to the right of the Timeline

Similar
This section provides an effective way of introducing you to new people to follow. If you're following a British comedian like Jimmy Carr, then you might enjoy keeping tabs on similar celebrities like Matt Lucas for example

Retweet
If you want to share someone's latest tweet with your own followers, click here and choose Retweet (or Quote Tweet) from the pop-up menu. This function enables particular news items or issues to get amazing publicity

Make a tweet
Click here to open the New Tweet window. Tap out anything you want to share using the iPad's keyboard. Potential followers can find you if your tweet contains topics that they are searching for

Knowledge base

Snowball effect

The Twitter app can be addictive. When you discover a favourite celebrity's Twitter feed, you can click on their Following link to see who they are interested in. Before you know it you're springing from one profile page to another, adding new people to follow. This gives you even more tweets to wade through in your Timeline every time you fire up the app. If you find people are less interesting than you'd expect (or if they stop tweeting altogether), then you can click the handy Unfollow button on their page.

03 Follow that star

To find folk to follow, click Search and type in a name. Each person's Twitter ID is prefaced with an @ symbol. If you want to follow the head writer of *Doctor Who*, for instance, then click on @steven_moffat to see their Twitter profile. Their bio should confirm that you've got the right person. Click Follow.

04 Explore

Once you've found people to follow click on the Timeline icon. The latest tweets from the people you follow will appear. Tap on a person's photo to see their profile. You can then click their Tweets icon to see all their recent tweets. Swipe the screen to move between various open profiles.

Using the Facebook app

If you have a Facebook account and don't want to bother using Safari to access it, there's an app that makes it much more compact. Here's how to use it

There are two benefits and one down side to using the official Facebook app as opposed to simply accessing the site using Safari. First, the disadvantage is that the app is currently designed for the iPod/iPhone so it appears in the middle of the iPad screen. Tap on 2X to double it up to iPad size. The advantages are that it is far better organised and easier to use than the actual website and also, the app uses notifications to let you know immediately about responses to your actions, posts on your wall or requests from friends. Once the Facebook app is downloaded and installed on your iPad, you simply need to enter your email address and Facebook password to get going. So now let's go see some of the functions that make accessing your account on the move as much fun as the main site.

"The Facebook app is far better organised and easier to use than the actual website"

Facebook Get friendly with this iPad app

01 Getting started

When the Facebook app is first run you will need to enter your email address and Facebook password to access your account. You'll notice that the first display which shows the News feed only fills the middle of the iPad screen. Tap on 2x to maximise the app.

02 Live news feeds

On the initial News feed page, there are five options. If you tap on Live Feed you can select from a range of notifications that you want displaying on this page instead. These include ones from Pages, Status updates, Photos, Links, Video, Notes and Groups. The page is updated as you scroll.

Quick access to your profile

Here's all the features that revolve around your personal profile

Enter your status
Type your status into this bar and it will appear on your profile. Your current and previous status updates, wall postings and comments from friends appear below

See all your photos
Check out all the images in all the folders that you have uploaded. Tap on the Photos panel to show the folders. Tap on a folder to see the pictures

Add a picture
Tap on the camera icon to upload a picture from your Photo Library and post it to your wall. After selecting the image you can then add a caption to it

Your personal details
If you tap on the Info panel at the bottom of the screen, your mobile phone, personal description, birthday, email address, interests and favourite things are all listed

Knowledge base
Notifications from Facebook
The Facebook app supports Push notifications. This means that when someone sends you a message, posts on your wall, asks to be a friend, tags you in a photo, posts an event or you get a friend confirmation, the Facebook server will send news of that to the app. If you aren't getting these then Push notifications are turned off. Tap on the Settings app and then on the Facebook app under Apps. Tap on Push Notifications. This gives a list of everything you can be notified for. They can all be toggled on or off.

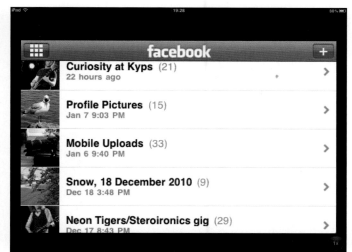

03 Post your status
The three options on the bar below the Facebook heading allow photos to be uploaded, your Status to be posted and to check in using Location services to show where you are. Tap on Status and enter what you are doing. Tap on Share when finished.

04 The main hub
Tap on the block of squares in the top left. This is the central hub of the Facebook app allowing access to all the website features including your Profile, Friends list, News feed, Messages, Places, Groups, Events, Chat and Notes. Tap Photos to see all the folders of images you have uploaded.

Essential app

A look at the essential apps that every iPad owner must download

140 The Elements: for UK and Ireland

141 Liquid Comics: Ramayan 3392AD, V1

142 Brushes iPad Edition

143 Epic Citadel

144 MaxJournal

145 Good Food Healthy Recipes for iPad, Tappy Memories

146 Chain Link HD

147 Grand Theft Auto: Chinatown Wars

148 Filterstorm 2

149 Faceover, Colors Pro

150 BBC News

151 USA Today

152 Drum Meister Grand, Red Bull BPM HD Player

153 Note Goal Pro, studio.HD

154 iFitness HD

155 Sky Sports News

156 CoPilot Live HD Europe

157 Urbanspoon, Wikihood for iPad

158 Air Display

159 Air Sketch, Atomic Web Browser

160 PocketMoney

161 Alarm Clock HD Free

162 IM+ Pro

163 Tweets, Dual Viewer For Facebook

164 NASA App, MathBoard

165 The World Factbook for iPad, WorldBook XL

Top pick
Epic Citadel

Top pick
Chain Link HD

Top pick
BBC News

Top pick
CoPilot Live HD Europe

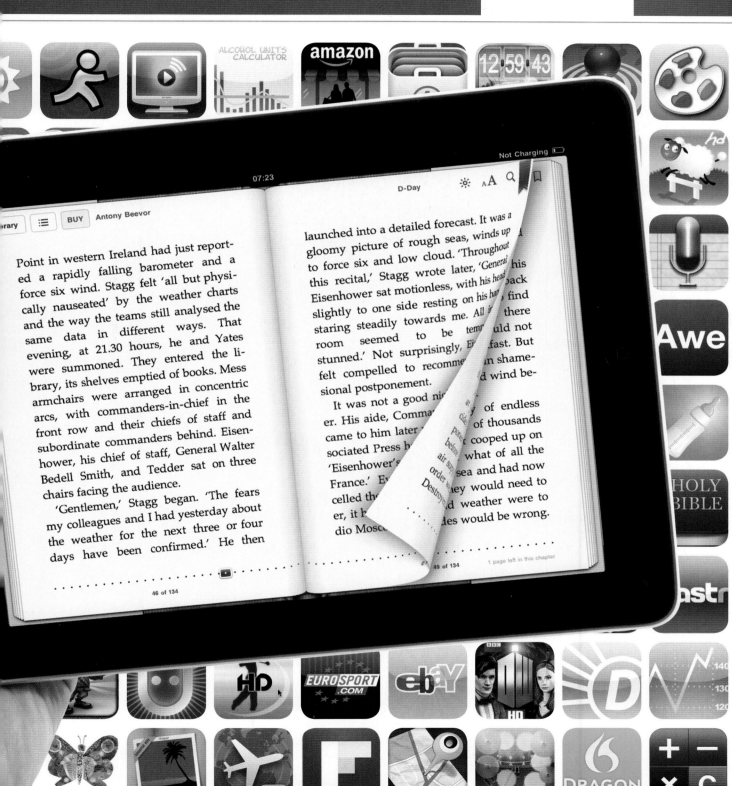

100 Essential Apps

We help you sort the wheat from the chaff in this comprehensive guide to the must-own apps for your iPad

With thousands of apps to choose from on the App Store, it can be quite daunting when deciding which ones to download, especially if you have to part with some hard-earned cash. The writer Theodore Sturgeon famously coined the adage, '90 per cent of everything is crud' – if this applies to apps then there's a real risk of wasting time and money downloading the wrong ones. It's annoying to fire up a recently bought app, realise it's not for you and then have to delete it from your iPad moments later, so this roundup will help you fill your device with apps that are useful, informative, and perhaps even life-saving!

To help you find 'keepers' for your iPad we've trawled the App Store and tested apps in its 20 categories. We'll introduce some great apps to help you work on the move so that you're no longer confined to word processing in the office. We'll show you which apps will keep you organised with day-to-day tasks so you can get things done, and discover the apps that will transform the most reluctant cook into a credible chef. We'll unveil some of the best book apps to keep you and your kids occupied and entertained, and then explore apps that let tone-deaf non-musicians make sweet music. We'll even reveal the best apps to keep you healthy, both physically and financially. Having the right apps on your iPad can transform your life in many ways, so read on to discover which ones we recommend and why.

Essential apps

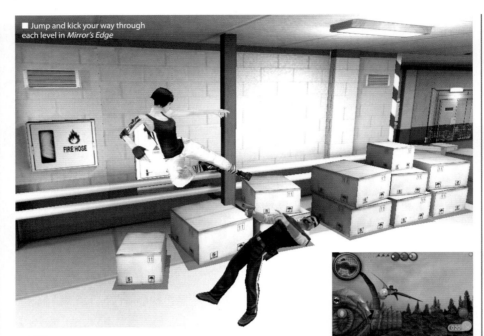

■ Jump and kick your way through each level in *Mirror's Edge*

Travel

When out and about you're bound to take your iPad with you, especially when it's packed full of apps designed to make your trip smoother. You can even track a friend's plane in flight when they're on holiday!

01 Google Earth Price: Free

 Tap in an address anywhere in the world and zoom in to an aerial view of that location in seconds.

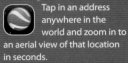

■ You can see your house!

02 FlightTrack Pro
Price: £5.99/$9.99

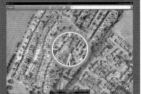 Watch the progress of planes in real time and keep tabs on specific flights – it's like a virtual air traffic controller.

03 Trip Advisor Price: Free

 Avoid hype and adverts by discovering people's genuine experiences of various flights, hotels and restaurants.

04 Open Table Price: Free

 Discover a good place to dine and then make a reservation, all from the comfort of this handy iPad app.

05 TravelJabs Price: Free

 Discover what inoculations you might need before a trip, so that you can safely enjoy exotic holidays.

■ Colour coding shows each destination's infection risks

Games

We've gone for games that are fun, addictive and easy to control with a swipe of a finger or a tilt of your iPad. *Mirror's Edge* lets you enjoy invigorating free running across an urban landscape as you leap from building to building, swing from girders and bash bad guys. The controls are ideal for the iPad as you can run and jump with a simple horizontal or vertical swipe. This perfect platformer will definitely get your pulse racing.

If you fancy a bit of variety, try the strategy game *Fieldrunners*, in which you tactically deploy weapons to stop the enemy crossing a field. The more enemies you kill, the more weapons you can buy. The sounds and graphics are of a very high quality and you can dive straight into the action.

Harbor Master HD is one of the most addictive games on the App Store. Use your finger to guide boats into various harbours, acquiring points for each crate they unload. At first it's oddly therapeutic

and satisfying, but as more and more boats fill the screen, it becomes harder to co-ordinate them while they dock, unload and disembark. Although a collision is inevitable, you'll find yourself replaying the game to try to beat your previous high score. Prepare to lose your iPad to your partner or kids if you let them play it!

Nanosaur 2 is perfect for the iPad. In this iPad version of the Mac classic, you make your pterodactyl swoop and soar by tilting the iPad in the appropriate direction. You can even enjoy networked multiplayer games like Capture the Flag via Apple's free Game Center app.

The popular *Doctor Who* franchise materialises on the App Store courtesy of *The Mazes Of Time*. In this puzzle-based game you control the Doctor and companion Amy Pond as they explore a variety of mazes while avoiding traps, unlocking doors and running away from a host of recognisable monsters like the Daleks and Cybermen. The gameplay can get a bit repetitive later on, but you do get to enjoy Murray Gold's excellent incidental music from the TV show.

■ Collect precious eggs in *Nanosaur 2*

■ Get lost at sea with this addictive game

■ Explore time and space with this *Doctor Who* puzzler

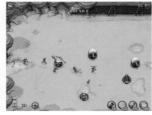

■ Fend off the enemy and upgrade your defensive weapons in *Fieldrunners*

Fieldrunners
For iPad
Price:
£4.99/$7.99

Harbor
Master HD
Price: Free

Doctor Who
Price:
£2.99/$4.99

Mirror's Edge
For iPad
Price:
£4.99/$9.99

Nanosaur 2
Price:
£2.39/$3.99

Entertainment

iQuarium HD
Price:
£1.19/$1.99

Aweditorium
Price: Free

TuneIn Radio
Price:
£0.59/$0.99

Plex
Price:
£2.99/$4.99

Air Video
Price:
£1.79/$2.99

Turn your iPad into a digital radio using TuneIn Radio and enjoy different stations from around the world. You can even record live shows and also stream podcasts.

Aweditorium is another innovative way to discover new music: explore by tapping on a thumbnail to launch a song, find out more info on the band and even download tracks straight from iTunes.

Once you've installed the Plex server software onto your Mac, you can then enjoy its music and movie content without filling up your iPad, and even stream content from online sources too. The Air Video app does a similar job, but with the advantage of having a free cut-down version that you can try out before committing any cash.

You can also take time out by launching iQuarium to enjoy the soothing movement of a virtual pet tropical fish. You can interact with your piscine pal by tapping on the screen and flicking gravel – don't forget to feed it though!

"Turn your iPad into a digital radio and enjoy stations from around the world"

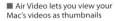

■ As time passes in iQuarium, you can unlock extra accessories

■ Air Video lets you view your Mac's videos as thumbnails

■ In Aweditorium, lyrics pop up to help you sing along

Books

Apps like Toy Story Read Along encourage kids to enjoy reading. As the narrator reads the text, the words become highlighted. You can record your own narration to personalise the experience, while video and audio clips are dropped in to add variety and keep the little ones entertained. The Heart And The Bottle is a beautifully illustrated story designed to get children interacting with the artwork as the story unfolds. Clicking and dragging on illustrations triggers animations to keep kids stimulated.

iBooks is Apple's book-reading app and the closest thing to reading a 'real' book. The pages curl as you drag to turn them and your collection is displayed on a bookshelf. You can also browse and download books from the iTunes Store. Kindle is another book reader that works in a similar way, though it isn't as pretty to look at as Apple's app. If you're after comic books, download and enjoy them using the marvellous Marvel Comics app.

■ Browse Amazon for bargain and cheap books

■ Turn a page by swiping and tap to add a bookmark

■ Read to your kids when you're not around

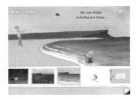

■ Use thumbnails to jump to a page in *The Heart And The Bottle*

iBooks
Price: Free

Kindle
Price: Free

Toy Story
Read Along
Price: Free

The Heart And
The Bottle
Price: £2.39

Marvel
Comics
Price: Free

Essential apps

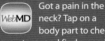

Health and fitness

These apps will help get you leaner, diagnose ailments and even soothe you to sleep. From calorie counters to workouts, there's an app for you.

01 Web MD Price: Free

Got a pain in the neck? Tap on a body part to check symptoms and find a possible cause and cure.

■ Touch the sore spot and discover possible causes of pain

02 Calorie Counter Price: Free

Fight the flab by counting the calories you eat. Discover food's nutritional values too for healthier eating.

03 Fitness Free HD Price: Free

Work out which exercises will enhance particular muscles. Packed with illustrated workouts to get you in shape.

04 My BMI Calculator Price: Free

Beautifully designed and simple to use. Swipe to enter height and weight values and find out your ideal BMI.

05 aSleep HD Price: £1.19/$1.99

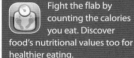

Soothe yourself to sleep by playing timer-controlled music. It takes a while to get the snore monitor going, though.

■ This app will sound an alarm to nip snoring in the bud

Lifestyle

Lifestyle apps can help you improve your life in a variety of ways, from helping you shop from the comfort of your iPad to showing you how to whistle up delicious home-cooked meals. Indeed, The Photo Cookbook enables the most inept or reluctant cook to produce delicious dinners. Using high-quality photos it takes you through the entire cooking progress step by step, from displaying a list of the ingredients you need to buy to showing photos of each step in progress. There are dozens of recipes to add to your repertoire. It's a must-have app if you want to impress friends and family with your new-found cooking skills.

If your meals are so good that you have to write about how amazing they are, then My Secret Diary enables you to record your thoughts on daily events. As well as attaching photos to your entries, you can even import music tracks from your iTunes Library to remind you of special times. To keep your thoughts and feelings secret you can add a lock code to your diary.

AroundMe is another Lifestyle app no one should be without. Using your current location, the app lets you know where the nearest banks, bars, petrol stations, hospitals and much more are located. With AroundMe you will always know where to find things in new towns, making it an exceptionally useful tool, wherever you may be.

The final Lifestyle app essential to your collection is eBay. The scary thing about using this app is how easy it becomes for you to buy things you didn't even know you wanted. If you browse for auctions that are ending soon it becomes hard to resist a spur-of-the-moment impulse buy. You could say the same for Amazon's Windowshop app – it lets you browse and buy anything from Blu-rays to beds.

The Photo Cookbook – Quick & Easy
Price: £2.99/$4.99

My Secret Diary
Price: Free

AroundMe
Price: Free

eBay
Price: Free

Windowshop
Price: Free

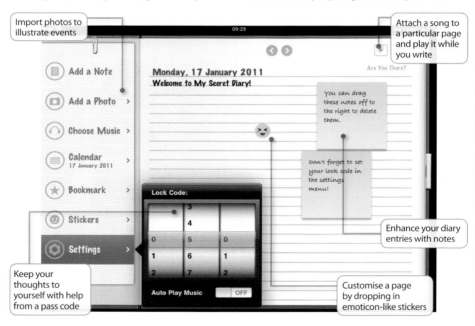

Import photos to illustrate events

Attach a song to a particular page and play it while you write

Keep your thoughts to yourself with help from a pass code

Enhance your diary entries with notes

Customise a page by dropping in emoticon-like stickers

■ Photo Cookbook clearly presents the ingredients you'll need

■ Watch items and pounce when the time is right

Social networking

1: AIM For iPad
Price: Free

2: FacemakrHD
Price:
£1.79/$2.99

3: Twitter
Price: Free

4: Friendly For
Facebook
Price: Free

5: Flipboard
Price: Free

The problem with social networking is that different friends use different ways of communicating – some prefer Google Chat, while others prefer to banter on Facebook. Thanks to AIM you can gather your mates under one app, discover who is online and message people on a variety of networks.

Many of you will use a photo to represent yourselves on networks like Facebook, but the slick and intuitively designed Facemakr Avatar Creator HD enables you to quickly knock up an eye-catching avatar to help you stand out from the crowd.

The official Twitter app provides a free and easy way to Tweet your thoughts or find interesting people to follow, while Facebook fans should also check out Friendly, an app that enables you to browse Facebook profiles and check out friends' photos in full screen. Flipboard is another handy app with an innovative design, which enables you to pop sites like Twitter and Facebook into squares and then launch them with a simple tap.

"Discover who is online and message people on a variety of networks"

■ Use AIM to chat to chums on an array of networks

■ You can also upload photos with Friendly

Photography

Although the iPad lacks a camera, you can still enjoy Photography apps. Quickly transfer shots from iPhone to iPad via Wi-Fi thanks to the amazing Photo Transfer – it saves you time and the hassle of routing the photos via your desktop computer. You can also use the iPad's comparatively large screen to fix photos using apps like PhotoGene, or turn them into paintings with ArtStudio. For inspiration and some pro photography tips, check out Guardian Eyewitness.

10 January 2011

■ Enjoy inspiring editorial images from around the world

The Guardian
Eyewitness
Price: Free

Flickpad Pro
Price:
£0.59/$0.99

PhotoGene
Price:
£2.39/$3.99

ArtStudio
Price:
£1.79/$2.99

Photo Transfer
Price:
£1.79/$2.99

■ Let Snooker Calc keep score while you focus on your long game

■ iRally is packed full of entertaining video clips

Sport

There's an app to suit every sporting enthusiast. Everyday Golf Coach may be a touch expensive, but it'll improve your performance at the fraction of the cost of a 'real' coach. Score more goals than the opposing team with the tactical wizardry of CoachPad, or tally up your score with Snooker Calc – just don't let anyone use your iPad as a beer mat! Alternatively, put your foot down and enjoy the thrills and spills offered by the World Rally Championship app.

Everyday Golf
Coach HD
Price:
£3.99/$6.99

Snooker Calc,
Price:
£0.59/$0.99

CoachPad
Price:
£2.99/$4.99

Eurosport
For iPad
Price: Free

iRally –
World Rally
Championship
Price: Free

Medical

There are apps designed to help us monitor lots of factors to help keep us healthy, from our daily blood pressure to the amount of alcohol we drink.

01 Baby Connect For iPad Price: £2.99/$4.99

Track every aspect of your baby's development, including growth, vaccinations and feeding.

02 Labor And Contraction Timer Price: Free

Log the duration of your contractions. It averages the timings for you, so you can work out when to head for the hospital.

03 iBP Blood Pressure Price: £0.59/$0.99

This doesn't measure pressure, but it enables you to record your readings so you can monitor your health over time.

04 Alcohol Units Calculator Price: £0.59/$0.99

Discover how many units of alcohol are in your drinks and log how many you have. It's easy to exceed

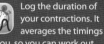

■ Find out how many units are in that beer before you buy one

05 Diabetes Buddy Price: £1.79/$2.99

Monitor your blood sugar levels and keep tabs on when you take your medication. It'll help you manage your condition.

■ Keep tabs on all the factors that can affect your blood sugar level

Essential apps

Finance

In these tight times it pays to watch your pennies. These apps will help you track the ups and downs of your portfolios and avoid being ripped off when converting currency.

01 Bloomberg Price: Free

Follow the rise and fall of the global and local stock markets and keep up to date on any financial news happenings.

02 Currency Convert Free
Price: Free

Scroll through countries and convert various currencies in seconds. This will help you avoid being ripped off.

■ Tap in the amount you want to convert and choose your currencies

03 My Student Budget Planner Price: Free

Avoid spending more than you can afford with this easy-to-use budgeting app. It also features tips on money management.

■ It's not just for students, mind

04 Account Tracker
Price: £1.79/$2.99

Keep a very tight grasp on your ins and outs so you spend less than you earn.

05 Stockwatch
Price: £3.49/$5.99

Customise this app to add your portfolio to its watch list and make informed decisions about what and when to buy and sell.

1: Quickoffice Connect Mobile Suite **Price:** £8.99/$14.99

2: Readdle Docs **Price:** £2.99/$4.99

3: AudioNote **Price:** £2.99/$4.99

4: Dragon Dictation **Price:** Free

5: Prompterous HD **Price:** Free

Business

Your iPad isn't just for playing games. Apps like Quickoffice Connect let you tap up a report or fill out a spreadsheet while out of the office, giving more freedom to work where and when you like. This means you can pop into a Wi-Fi-enabled coffee shop, edit your documents and export them via email or pop them in a dropbox for colleagues to collect. If you want to read different kinds of document (like PDFs or Word files, for example) then you'll need ReaddleDocs. It'll also let you browse mail from various sources and access attachments.

"These essential apps mean business!"

Too tired to type? Then simply let Dragon Dictation turn your speech into text! Or you may prefer to jog your memory using Audio Note. Apps like Prompterous HD can help you improve your public speaking, whether in a presentation or making a speech at a wedding. These essential apps mean business!

■ Open and edit documents and spreadsheets on the go

Productivity

If you tend to procrastinate or have trouble multitasking, then these apps will help you get things done – and on time too. There are apps to make typing easy, like IA Writer, or you can scribble notes and drawings as if you were wielding a pen, courtesy of Penultimate. Keep productive with to-do list app Sorted, and produce more complex multimedia presentations and documents using Apple's powerful and slickly designed Pages and Keynote apps.

■ Position and scale content by sliding and pinching in Keynote

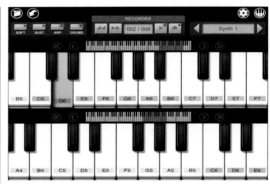

■ Enjoy a variety of different keyboard layouts

Music

If you enjoy listening to or making music then these apps deserve a place on your iPad. Classically trained players will love Pianist Pro with its range of different keyboard sounds, while the non-trained musician should check out the amazing MorphWiz and create synthesised sound loops by simply stroking the screen. Discover the artists behind a specific track using Shazam, listen to music via Spotify, then enjoy the videos courtesy of Vevo HD.

Sorted
Price:
£0.59/$0.99

Pages
Price:
£5.99/$9.99

Keynote
Price:
£5.99/$9.99

IA Writer
Price:
£2.99/$4.99

Penultimate
Price:
£0.59/$0.99

MorphWiz
Price:
£5.99/$9.99

Shazam for iPad
Price: Free

Pianist Pro
Price:
£5.99/$9.99

VevoHD
Price: Free

Spotify
Price: Free

A Deep Bench of Leadership at Apple

■ *New York Times* stories pop up in a scrollable bar

News

■ Download your favourite *Sunday Times* sections

Many news providers share stories as RSS feeds. This makes apps like MobileRSS essential, as you can gather your favourite news feeds into one place for quick and easy access. Alternatively, if you like your news delivered with a particular political slant, you should check out apps like *Sunday* or *New York Times*. Read It Later lets you bookmark interesting articles on your Safari browser and read them offline at a more convenient time, and if you're into sci-fi then Blastr will feed your news need.

Read It Later Pro **Price:** £1.79/$2.99

Blastr **Price:** Free

MobileRSS **Price:** Free

Sunday Times **Price:** Free

NYTimes **Price:** Free

Navigation

Your iPad may be limited when it comes to navigation if it's dependent on a Wi-Fi connection, but many apps will still be useful on an unconnected device. Before visiting a foreign city you can download a map on ForeverMap or City Maps 2Go, then explore your destination without being connected. Trails – GPS Tracker allows you to import routes directly onto your iPad, and you can even track ships with Ship Finder HD!

■ Hold the iPad flat for a 2D compass in Sun & Moon…

■ Download OpenStreet Maps for a host of countries

Sun & Moon Compass HD **Price:** £1.19/$2.99

City Maps 2Go **Price:** £1.19/$2.99

Ship Finder HD **Price:** £4.99/$7.99

Trails – GPS Tracker **Price:** £2.39/$3.99

ForeverMap **Price:** £2.39/$4.99

Weather HD **Price:** £0.59/$0.99

Weather ProHD **Price:** £2.99/$4.99

Weather+ Free **Price:** Free

Accu Weather **Price:** £0.59/$0.99

Aquarium Clock – Weather Forecast **Price:** Free

Weather

Here's our pick of the best weather apps, although you won't need all of them as they do a similar job. Weather HD gives you the basic forecast, but for more in-depth information – including satellite images – cough up for WeatherPro HD. Aquarium Clock is a novelty clock app that overlays a forecast against an aquarium backdrop, and Weather+ Free and Accu Weather also do excellent jobs of getting you the forecast.

■ You can pay £2.99 to upgrade to the full version of Weather+

Night Stand HD **Price:** £1.19/$1.99

Convert **Price:** £0.59, $0.99

Calculator Pro For iPad **Price:** Free

Living Earth HD **Price:** £0.59/$0.99

App Shopper **Price:** Free

Utilities

The Utilities section of the App Store contains a wide range of handy apps that enable your iPad to fulfil a variety of useful functions, such as an alarm clock and world clock. As the iPad doesn't come equipped with a calculator it's essential to include one of those, and we recommend complementing your calculator with a handy unit converter. There's even an app to help you find free or bargain-price apps, making it a must-have addition to your app collection!

■ Add other cities to see their time and weather with Night Stand HD

■ Discover what time it is for those abroad with the world clock in Living Earth HD

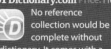
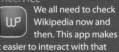
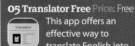

Price: £7.99/$12.99 **Developer:** Element Collection

The Elements: for UK and Ireland

If only science at school was as interactive and slickly presented as this

Make science and chemistry come alive on your iPad, with this app based on hard-backed, bestseller, *The Elements* by Theodore Gray. A fuller title would be 'The Elements of the Periodic Table', but then you are given no real introduction or background to the table, it's just presented in its full glory and it's your job to go investigate. Well, that's once you eventually download the app because (are you sitting down?) it's a whopping 1.7GB in size! Pray for a fast connection and hope to have enough room on your iPad for it.

Really, this is far too large and the developers should look at optimising their graphics to make it smaller. One saving would be to ditch the inane animated song that comes up when the app first runs. On with the show: by tapping on an element you will bring up a rotating 3D picture of a sample along with a swathe of facts and figures. Tap on individual elements of the text and you'll be presented with more brain-stretching statistics powered by the WolframAlpha computational engine. You can even find out the price of gold.

For students, it's useful to see the sources for the stats listed as an option for further investigation. This is all pretty hardcore, but a second screen of text lightens up the science talk with background information. It has to be said that this is popular science, aimed at school kids, rather than the brain-hurting technical detail of the first page, so expect anecdotes and asides in among the facts. What really makes this app come into its own are the practical uses shown for each element.

Some elements have video clips of experiments showing what they are used for, and if that doesn't inspire you then perhaps bringing an element up full screen will. Double tap it again and it turns into a 3D image. Get yourself some 3D glasses (not the red-cyan or cinema ones) to see the image jump off the page. Now, there's much discussion about how sharp the graphics are but the reality is that some of them are and some aren't. Also, the photographer

really needed to work on his depth of field because edges of numerous objects go out of focus as they rotate. Still, the facts should keep students happy, the informal descriptions make it accessible for everyone, and the plentiful graphics make it an attractive app to show around.

Rating ★★★★★

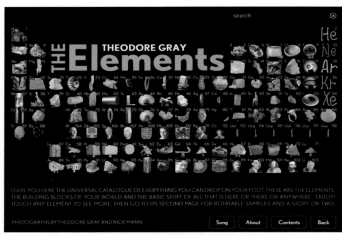

■ The full Periodic Table containing all the elements. Did you want background information to the app? Hard luck, just tap and go

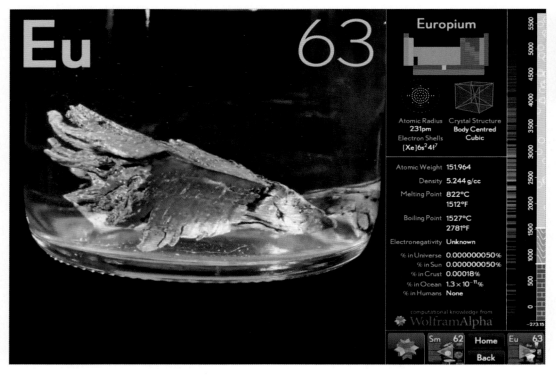

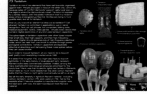

■ It's the second page of text that contains the light-hearted, yet fact filled information on the element. The 'typical uses' illustrations are very handy

■ Spinning graphics are the norm but the pretty effects are backed up by the WolframAlpha computational engine on this page

Price: £5.99/$9.99 **Developer:** MacOligarch

Liquid Comics: Ramayan 3392AD, V1

The ancient mythological fantasy updated for the 21st Century world

Well there's some history with this gargantuan download – 500Mb+ of precious storage needed. *Ramayan 3392AD* is based upon the ancient Indian epic of Ramayana but it's been re-imagined as a post-apocalyptic story set in the far future.

This new version uses all the traditional character names but they are worked into completely new stories. The concept was first released by Virgin Comics, covering eight issues and three compendium volumes in print form, and became hugely popular.

This updated version is subtitled Volume 1 and covers 205 Technicolor iPad pages. If you're unfamiliar with the stories – the history, characters and names particularly – there are two great primers which can be downloaded for free and are worth checking out. It's actually recommended that you read *Guide Book* and *Origins* first, however, so that you can get a good grounding of this wonderful fantasy world.

In a nutshell the story is science fantasy: the Earth has been devastated, mankind has been virtually obliterated and the evil Ravan is on course to take out what little humanity is left with the help of his evil hordes. Technology combines with swords and sorcery in Ravan's physical make up; he is able to shape-shift because he's made of sentient nanites, called Yantra.

The format is portrait, rotating to landscape just gives you a very small portrait format. It's possible to zoom in so that the landscape format is wide enough to read the text comfortably and then scroll down the screen.

There's not a lot to the app in itself, just an intro to the five main characters and then into the comic itself. This is all presented and reads in typical graphic novel style and you'll soon see where the storage space has gone with the sumptuous and detailed illustrations. The only real disappointment is that a modest amount of zooming in results in the illustrations becoming soft and not really revealing any more detail. Despite this they don't have pixilated edges. As far as the text style goes, don't worry if you think it's going to be unreadable, high fantasy speak. There's plenty of banter and modern, Western idioms. Also, when a traditional phrase or expression is used, there's usually a handy boxout with a translation in that frame. The only issue is assimilating the place names but with perseverance you'll discover this really is an epic story updated for modern tastes and the graphics really do show off your iPad's capabilities to its best. In terms of value it's a little on the expensive side, so do check out those primers first. A great read and a very cool app.

Rating ★★★★★

■ (Right) Bit of a Braveheart moment here. You'll soon feel at home with the characters and the modern styling

■ (Left) The opening screen gives background info on five main characters before you start on the story itself

Price: £4.99/$7.99 **Developer:** Steve Sprang

Brushes iPad Edition

Become a master art without ever touching a paintbrush

It's rare that iPad apps continually make the world news, but this amazing package from Steve Sprang is no ordinary, thrown together, cash cow app. It was featured in newspapers around the world when David Kassan was using it to create amazing lifelike portraits of New York residents – Google his name and you'll see what this little piece of kit is capable of. Due to its ease of use and great results, it's constantly been at the top of the App Store charts and has even been used to produce numerous covers for the New Yorker.

Of course, once you start using this delightful piece of kit you'll soon realise why it's been getting all its critical acclaim. For you see, Brushes is quite simply the best art package we've currently discovered on Apple's online service and it's an absolute joy to use. While we'll admit to not being the most artistic of people, it's still amazing just what you can achieve with Brushes in a relatively short amount of time. This in part is due to its sheer ease of use and the insane amount of excellent options that you have available at your finger tips. There are 19 virtual brushes to use, you can work over six high definition layers and use five different blend modes to add even more depth to your pictures. Zooming in and out is incredibly simple to do, you can import your own photos and manipulate them as you see fit and even use a VGA/TV output to show off your works of art as you create them on a larger eternal screen.

The iPad screen itself, however, is absolutely perfect for this kind of thing, especially when compared to similar apps available on Apple's smaller devices, and as such you have the space and clarity to really see what you are creating with ease. With no brush, stylus or other mediator between you and the picture, it really feels like you are in control, and using your finger to paint is a very slick control mechanism that feels extremely natural.

Another useful touch is that Flickr support is included, allowing you to easily upload any of your masterpieces online for all to see. There's even a handy replay mode that redraws your paintings. All in all it's a wonderful little package that is an absolute bargain at its asking price, and is so much more sophisticated than finger painting. It's perfect for the kids too; load it up while your stuck in a doctor's waiting room, or if your train is delayed and they'll be happy for hours.

If we wanted to be churlish we could complain that Brushes is geared more towards existing artists, and as a result is not very accessible to beginners – there's no help file for example – and you can't always see what you're drawing when using a small brush, but we're just being picky here. Brushes is a truly superb app available at a ridiculously good price. The results can be exceptional if you have the artistic flair to go alongside this app, but even newcomers will find much to enjoy here. Regardless of whether you're just the occasional doodler or a full time artist, however, we guarantee that you'll fall in love with this excellent little app.

Rating ★★★★★

■ We did this after just five minutes of playing with brushes and colours. We've already sold it online for an absolute fortune

■ Enhance your stored photographs with your own artistic touch

Price: Free   **Developer:** Epic Games

Epic Citadel

Epic by name epic by nature

Epic Games has built up an incredible reputation in the games industry since its debut in 1991. Famed for hits like *Gears Of War* and the *Unreal* series, its reach within the industry extends even further due to its excellent Unreal Engine middleware software that many developers use.

While best known for its PC and Xbox support the developer is now setting its sights on the iPad and iPhone and its first venture on the software is suitably epic. However, let's get one thing straight, Epic Citadel is not a game of any sort, more an actual experience. It's basically nothing more than a tech demo, designed by Epic to show off just how powerful its engine is. Worry not though, for while there are no enemies to kill or objectives to complete it's one of the most atmospheric experiences to be found on Apple's machine.

Once the title screen is out of the way you're simply presented with a huge medieval marketplace. Movement can be controlled by simply touching the screen and moving in the direction you want to go, or you can use an extremely sensitive dual-stick shooter method that makes navigating the impressive world an absolute breeze.

The scale of Epic Citadel is sensational. Move outside the huge marketplace and you can see far off into the horizon. Best of all, everything you can see is reachable – providing you're prepared to spend time walking there – it looks utterly beautiful and reveals just what is possible with a little time and effort. Buildings feature incredibly detailed brickwork, the floors of a nearby church are so polished you can see reflections in them, while the many lighting effects on offer are astounding. If that wasn't enough the entire demo is silky smooth, ensuring that first-person shooters and titles like *Oblivion* could easily find a proper home on the iPad.

While there's nothing really to do in the demo, you'll be happy just walking around the empty, but enchanting world. If you have a friend who laughs at the iPad's capabilities compared to handheld gaming systems, just get them to spend ten minutes on this. They'll never dare to mock your expensive device again.

■ Remember in *Halo* when you looked at the grass? This is far more impressive. You'll be in awe!

Rating ★★★★★

Price: £1.79/$2.99 **Developer:** Omaxmedia

MaxJournal

This diary app transforms your iPad into an elegant daily journal

Diary apps tend to fall into two categories – there's the personal assistant style of app that organises your appointments and schedules. Then there's the more relaxed type, based around the kind of journal in which some of us like to record the ins and outs of our day at its close, preferably with a nice hot drink and a curled-up pet snoozing somewhere nearby.

MaxJournal definitely falls into this second category, the design revolving around a virtual large-format journal of the type that can be found in expensive stationery shops. This instantly imbues it with an air of quality, oozing the sort of luxurious finger-appeal which makes it a pleasure to use.

The main interface consists of a large central page area with a dateline across the top which is also used for accessing the year and the month. Accompanying this is a set of small tabs down the left-hand side, each of which bears a date. When tapped, each tab brings up a whole page that corresponds to that day, ready to be filled with your thoughts and accounts of your exploits.

A cluster of buttons found on the upper right of the screen handles features such as: the comprehensive Export and Backup options, a search feature that can target specific words within your entries, the online help system and the font. Also handy is a password protection setting where you can protect your thoughts from nosey family. Photos and tags can be added, scrapbook style, in a panel on the right of the screen, and a large 'Today' button rounds things off, allowing you to zip right to the current day's page with a single touch.

Tap a page and it zooms instantly to fill the iPad's screen, tap once more and up pops the keyboard ready to make an entry. There is a choice of 16 different fonts of variable size, old favourites such as Helvetica and Marker Felt Wide being joined by more esoteric choices like Journal and Kayleigh, which lend a more handwritten feel to jottings.

Other than changing the size and font however, there seem to be no other text style formatting options available, a shame as it would be nice to be able to use Bold and Italic styles for extra expressive entries. Overall, MaxJournal is one of the best of this type of app that we've seen.

Rating ★★★★★

■ The main interface is uncluttered and efficient, getting you to your entries quickly

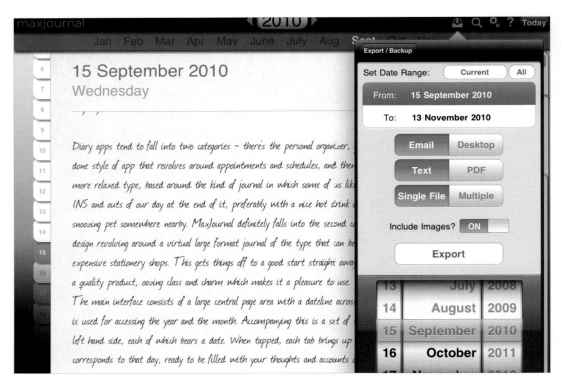

■ Each entry in your journal can be accompanied by up to three photos

■ MaxJournal's excellent export and backup options include a variable date range

■ Here we learn all about blueberries – one of ten healthy ingredients given extra attention

Price: £2.39/$3.99 **Developer:** BBC Worldwide

Good Food Healthy Recipes for iPad

Get into healthy eating, iPad style

As far as recipes go, there can't be many more trusted resources than the BBC's Good Food website, and this app brings together over 150 recipes with a bias towards the healthier side of eating. As a consequence, each recipe contains a breakdown of all the relevant nutritional information, such as calories, protein and fat content.

The variety of dishes on offer is wide – you'll find healthier versions of chicken korma and chocolate mocha cake, rubbing shoulders with combinations you might not have tried, such as ginger and lime chicken with sweet potato mash. Attention to detail is high, with a choice offered between metric or imperial units and a cooking timer accessible from every page of the app. Recipes can be favourited for quick retrieval, or shared with friends via email, and there are also ten video clips demonstrating various cooking skills. The interface is clean, modern, well laid out and easy to navigate, with stunning photos throughout, so if you're looking to start eating more healthily, shedding a couple of pounds for this would be a good start.

Rating ★★★★☆

■ Photo and audio notes can be added to enhance your answers

Price: £0.59/$0.99 **Developer:** El-Hitamy I & T LLC

Tappy Memories

Go crazy with loops, add effects and create arrangements

Using Tappy Memories is a bit like having a version Eamonn Andrews on your iPad, interviewing you about your life. You're presented with a series of questions, some of them quite candid and thought-provoking – 'What's your favourite memory of your father?' is one example – which you can answer as fully or concisely as you like, and even attach relevant photos and add audio notes to further illustrate things.

Questions can be customised, and once you've completed the questionnaire, or got somebody else to answer the questions instead, the results can be shared via email as a PDF document that reads a bit like a 'This Is Your Life' dossier. This will contain only text and photos, as at the time of writing there is no way to export any audio files that you create within the app, which is a shame. That said, as a way of nudging you into writing down precious memories that might otherwise never be shared, Tappy Memories is one of those rarest of things – a totally original idea, and for that alone it should be applauded.

Rating ★★★★☆

Essential apps

Price: £1.19/$1.99 Developer: Joshua Levine

Chain Link HD

Proof that inventive puzzle games still exist on the iPad

 With so many clever puzzle games on the iPad you really need to ensure that yours will stand apart from the crowd. Rather than produce yet another Match 3 or physics clone, Joshua Levine has instead created a concept that while deceptively easy to learn, becomes virtually impossible to put down.

A swirling vortex sits at the centre of the screen and is surrounded by a variety of different shaped icons. By using your fingers you have to drag the shapes into the vortex's centre which will net you points. You'll get more points for linking the same shapes together, but in doing so you'll possibly create an ever increasing chain, which, should it hit a different type of object, will instantly rob you of a life. Needless to say, things begin to get increasingly tricky as your desire to create huge point-scoring chains is continually tempered by the potential loss an unplanned collision will cause. To make matters more frantic you only have a set amount of time to clear each stage, meaning you'll need a deft mind and even defter fingers to ensure you reach your goal in time.

While the core gameplay mechanics are perfectly sound, Levine has added a number of different gameplay modes to ensure that there's always a reason to return to his entertaining game. Timed mode features either a simple 60-second score attack mode or gives you a set amount of time to score a certain number of points, while Arcade mode has you scoring as many points as you can before a single collision. Add in a selection of power-ups and individual challenges that appear as you play the game and Chain Link HD becomes a thoroughly gripping experience that will keep you glued to your iPad.

The real beauty of Chain Link HD, however, is its glorious controls. While available on the iPhone, its small screen makes it something of a nightmare to play. There's no issue on the iPad though, and the larger screen and multi-touch controls turn it into a completely different experience, especially as it's much easier to drag around two different shaped chains at the same time.

Add in Open Feint support and some incredibly slick presentation and Chain Link HD very easily justifies its bargain asking price. This really is a fantastic little puzzler that proves novel ideas are still coming thick and fast on Apple's machine.

Rating ★★★★☆

■ If different coloured shapes collide then you're going to lose one of your precious lives

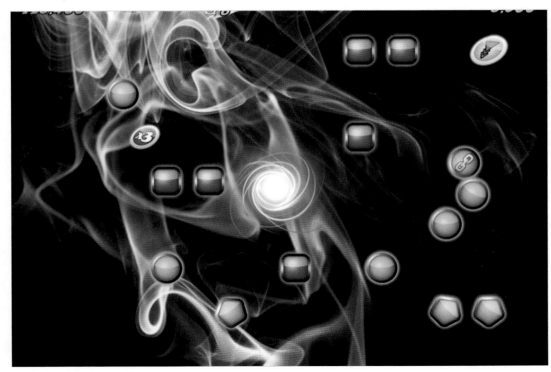

■ While linking chains grants you more points, there's more chance that you'll hit something and lose a life quite quickly

■ There are plenty of power-ups on offer, so be sure to collect them all as they can drastically affect the gameplay

Price: £5.99/$8.99 **Developer:** Rockstar Leeds

Grand Theft Auto: Chinatown Wars

And you thought the iPhone version was good…

This is the fourth version of *GTA: Chinatown Wars* that Rockstar Games released. After making its debut on the DS, it eventually moved over to both the PSP and iPhone. This version, while little different to its smaller iPhone brother, is arguably the better version and despite the fact that we have already completed the latter, we once again dived into the seedy world that Rockstar Leeds has so meticulously created.

After his father's death Huuang Lee is charged with delivering their family sword to his uncle who plans to use it to retain control of the many Triad gangs of Liberty City. As soon as he arrives, however, Lee is immediately accosted and loses the precious weapon. What follows is a seemingly bog-standard tale of revenge. Except of course it's anything but. While Rockstar has churned out very similar stories for virtually every one of its *GTA* games, it also has an eye for great dialogue and cinematic twists. As a result the tale of *Chinatown Wars* may be a story you've heard many times before, but it's all kept fresh and exciting thanks to solid narrative and enjoyable characters.

There is more to *GTA* games than solid stories, however, and *Chinatown Wars* proves to be just as competent on the gameplay front. Clever scenes slowly introduce you to all the gameplay mechanics, and Rockstar has also wisely enabled you to fiddle around with controls layouts to allow you to make use of the iPad's bigger screen. As a result there's none of the clumsiness that could be found in the iPhone version and you'll soon be hitching cars, running drugs and shooting bad guys like a seasoned pro. Admittedly the virtual controls aren't quite as solid as those on other handhelds, but the touch screen is utilised incredibly well allowing you to do everything from jacking cars to assembling sniper rifles with a few deft taps and swipes of the screen.

The gameplay throughout is exceptionally good, and Rockstar has included plenty of variety – including a surprisingly deep drug running strategy game – to ensure there's always something to do in its forbidden city. Add in some truly glorious high-res visuals that really show off the squalor of Liberty City – with only the odd frame rate dip here and there – and *Chinatown Wars* becomes another essential addition to your iPad library.

Rating ★★★★☆

What a place! Beaten up, shot and nearly drowned - within minutes of getting here.

■ The superb cut-scenes look even more cinematic on the iPad's lush screen

■ The touchscreen is used in a variety of inventive ways throughout *Chinatown War*'s gripping story

■ Driving feels much more responsive this time around, far better than it did on the iPhone. While the larger screen allows you to enjoy the visuals more

Price: £2.39/$3.99 **Developer:** Tai Shimizu

Filterstorm 2

Edit your photos with expert effects while on the move

The name of this app doesn't really portray its actual use. Filterstorm suggests a range of brash and perhaps naff effects that can be used to bling up your photos. That couldn't be further from the truth, though; the one thing Filterstorm doesn't offer is filters, at least not in that way. What it does do, however, is allow you to make subtle adjustments to images in a way that users of the desktop version of Photoshop will be familiar with.

You can alter a photo's luminance, hue, saturation, colour temperature and sharpness by picking from the menu to the left of the screen. Some settings are made with slider bars while others actually allow you to alter the curves of the image using a graph. This is particularly useful if you want to correct colour casts or change the feel of a photograph.

And what's really impressive is that you can apply masks so that you can choose exactly what part of a photo you want to alter. So, for instance, if you want to darken a blue sky, you can change the colour of just that part of the photo, while leaving the foreground untouched. The same applies to, say, a portrait – you can warm skin tones without spoiling the background.

Once you've made a successful edit, you can save it as an 'Automation', which allows you to apply the same changes to subsequent photographs.

In addition, the app also offers more regular editing tools, such as crop, rotate and straighten – all of which are self-explanatory. The only gimmicky effects are vignette and posterize tools, which seem at odds with the rest of the app.

Our only real gripe with Filterstorm 2 is that the white on black interface isn't the most polished of looks, but that doesn't detract from its usability. All in all, though, Filterstorm is a very powerful tool but you do need to know what you're doing. Even if you're an experienced image manipulator, it's

well worth watching the excellent tutorial videos beforehand to learn how to control the app. Filterstorm is not a quick fix but rather an app you have to spend time getting to know; do that and you will see your photo editing improving no end.

Rating ★★★★★

■ A menu on the left gives access to the many editing tools. Don't let the interface put you off

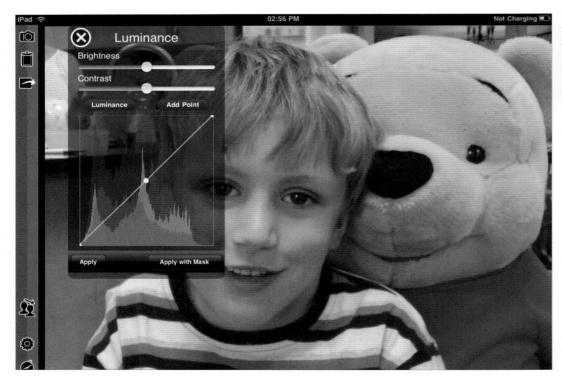

■ Once you've completed your edit you can save it as an Automation so it can be applied to other images

■ Being able to adjust the curves of an image lets you dial out colour casts

Price: £1.19/$1.99 **Developer:** Revelary LLC

Faceover

Photo face manipulation that gives great results

This isn't the only face-swap app available but it's certainly one of the best. It's simple to use, has a good interface and the results can be very convincing. Once you've chosen a photo, you move a selection oval over a person's face and carefully adjust the size, shape and orientation of the oval to fit. You'd expect this to be done using pinch gestures but, instead, you use the controls around the oval, which works well.

Then, you simply drag the person's face to where you want it – usually onto another person – and drop it into place. It's as simple as that. Some of the icons across the top of the screen aren't self-explanatory but a help menu steps in to, well, help.

At first, this app appears to be for fun. However, if you're careful you can also use it as a serious editing tool. For instance, if you have a group portrait where someone is blinking, you can copy and paste that person's face from another shot. Or you may want to replace that dumped boyfriend/girlfriend with your latest date. The possibilities are endless! Faceover is a great little app that could really improve your photos, while also being rather fun.

■ The selector oval is easy to position and size, while the help menu explains the icons

Rating ★★★★★

Price: £1.19/$1.99 **Developer:** Happio Workshop

Colors Pro

Bring colour back to black and white

You've surely seen photos that are part colour and part black and white. Back in the old days, artists would painstakingly add colour to black and white prints. Then, when computers came along, it was possible to take a photo and selectively remove the colour from it but, working with a mouse, it could be a fiddly process.

Colors Pro embraces touch screen technology to make it easy for anyone to add or remove colour from their images. When you load a photo, it appears in monochrome, and you simply run your finger over the areas you want to be in colour. If you make a mistake, tap the undo button or shake the iPad.

There's also the option of selecting areas with rectangle, circle and lasso tools but, to be honest, the rubbing through method is best. You can also work the other way, rubbing out the colour from a photo, although that's not the default setting. Colors Pro does just the one job, but it does it well.

"Run a finger over bits you want in colour"

Rating ★★★★★

■ The finished result is easy to achieve. You can save it or email it

■ Beginning with a black and white photo, you can 'rub' through to make the colour magically appear

Price: Free **Developer:** BBC Worldwide

BBC News

The world's largest news provider, on your iPad

The BBC is a well-respected news provider all around the world and has established a massive online presence with its excellent website too.

The news section of the BBC website is available via a free app that makes good use of the iPad. When held in landscape mode, you browse through thumbnails of top stories on the left half of the screen (you can scroll sideways through each row of thumbnails to reveal more). Tap a story to read it in full on the right-hand side. Turning the iPad to the vertical format enlarges the main story and leaves a ribbon of thumbnails along the top.

Most stories have at least one still image within them, and many have video embedded too. Tap on a video and it plays full screen.

You can personalise what appears in the story previews by editing the categories. So, you may want to keep up with, say, World news, UK news, Technology, and Entertainment and Arts, while ignoring items that feature Politics, Health and Sport. It could be argued that such self-censorship makes you closed-minded but it is certainly nice to have the option to cater to your tastes and interests.

Unlike the BBC website, the app doesn't give headlines – each preview is the same size – so you don't have to rely on a news editor's opinion on what's newsworthy. That said, there is a 'Top Story' section which, unlike the others, can't be hidden.

Also, a ticker strip, much like you see on many TV news programmes, also displays the latest news but, oddly, you can't click on these to get the full story.

All in all, this is an excellent app, although we would like to see the ability to fill the screen with a thumbnail preview of stories and then, when one is selected, for the full story to then be full screen. As it is, in landscape mode the screen is always split 50-50 between previews and a selected story, which is a bit of a shame really.

Added value comes in the form of the ability to watch the BBC News Channel live from within the app. As you'd expect, resolution is low to ensure steady steaming but, on the plus side, you can pause the programme and rewind it by 30 seconds. Strictly speaking, you need a television licence to watch this, something that is mentioned in the app's help section.

To keep up with current affairs, this is a must-have for any iPad user – and unbeatable value, too.

Rating ★★★★★

■ In landscape mode, there are preview thumbnails on the left and the selected story to the right. You can choose what categories appear in the previews

■ The vertical screen has more space for the main story with a ribbon of previews above

■ You can watch the BBC News Channel live from within the app, so long as you have a reasonable internet connection to hand

Price: Free   Developer: USA Today

USA Today

Showing the way forward for electronic newspapers

Amazingly, the United States didn't have a national daily newspaper until 1982, when *USA Today* was launched. Always a mould-breaking publication, the paper was one of the first to use full colour photographs and has a concise, sensible and informative writing style. As you'd expect, the content is very US-centric but there's still plenty to interest people in other countries.

The *USA Today* app is a lesson in adopting a daily newspaper to the iPad platform, and the fact that it's free is astonishing. The front page is divided into sections, with the main news one being scrollable, so you can see at a glance what's happening in the world (or rather in America). Tap a story and it fills the screen so that it's easy and clear to read, with an occasional photo breaking up the text.

You can then scroll sideways from story to story, just as you would flick through the pages of a printed paper. To return to the front page you tap an icon on the top left, which could be a bit larger. When back at the start, tapping the masthead brings up the paper's various sections, each with its own clear front page.

There's even a crossword page, which may not be as taxing as British cryptic puzzles (actually, it's very simple), but it is nicely adapted for the iPad and includes a timer, the option to highlight mistakes, and access to previous days' puzzles, not to mention a naughty 'Hints' button.

An 'In Pictures' section utilises the iPad's superb screen to treat you to superb photography of current events that are pickable from a range of photo galleries.

It's a good app, but it's not quite perfect. It does tend to crash on a regular basis, but this could be down to other factors, including the hardware we tested the app on. Also, there's no way to see the contents of an issue at a glance; a pop-up ribbon menu would be welcome. Still, you can't complain, as the app is free and gives access to some good quality journalism presented on the iPad in a sensible, no frills fashion.

Rating ★★★★★

■ Crosswords are simple to solve while the interface is pleasant to use

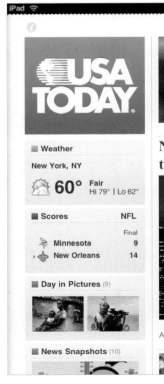

■ Various sections of the paper can be accessed by tapping the masthead. Each section has its own front page

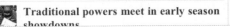

■ The front page displays news headlines, and you need to scroll through the main section to see more

Essential apps

Price: £1.19/$1.99 **Developer:** greySox

Drum Meister Grand
Unleash your inner Stewart Copeland with a virtual drum kit

The iPhone has revitalised the market for fingertip drum kit apps, which really come into their own when given the larger screen of the iPad to expand into. The extra space makes the virtual drum heads so much easier to hit, and the idea of having a virtual drum kit on a mobile touchscreen device suddenly starts to make a lot more sense.

Such is the case with Drum Meister Grand, the iPad-specific version of greySox' popular fingertip kit emulator. The included Rock, Jazz, Electro and Dance kits are generously appointed, each with four toms, a splash cymbal, standard crash and a crash/ride. The drums can be freely arranged over the playing area, so if you prefer your hi-hat cymbal to the right of the snare, just drag it into its new position. The samples are generally very good, and latency is down to a tolerable level, making this one of the more playable apps of its kind. Indeed, playing along to songs from your iTunes library becomes so addictive, it's a wonder this review ever actually got written!

This is a great little music simulator that will have seasoned drummers tapping out beats with their fingertips and newcomers learning rhythm on the move.

■ Extra drums can be added and auto-roll triggers set up from here

Rating ★★★★☆

Price: £18.49/$30.99 **Developer:** Red Bull Media House

Red Bull BPM HD Player

Why lug a crate of CDs to your next DJ gig, when you can take your iPad?

■ Pitch adjustment slider range is switchable between +/- 4, 8, 16 & 100%

Red Bull is marketing this app as a serious DJ mixer app suitable for club use, as reflected in its hefty price tag. After a quick go, you get the sense that the price might be justified; it's brimming with advanced features and very easy to use. Beatcounting, BPM sync, hot cueing and pitch nudge buttons are all present, and the interface design would look perfectly at home in a DJ booth.

If the high price has you wavering, a free version is available that includes four fixed tracks. Upgrading to the full version allows you free rein to import and mix any tune from your iTunes library. The fact that the iPad only has one physical audio output can be overcome in two ways: Red Bull has a separate £5.99 Master Out app that transmits the main output of BPM HD Player to another device over Wi-Fi, or alternatively an optional headphone splitter is available for £8.50 from the Red Bull website. Overall, impressive stuff.

"Red Bull BPM HD Player is brimming with advanced features"

■ Red Bull gives you wings. This app gives you the Ting Tings

Rating ★★★★☆

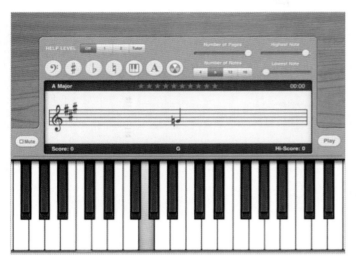

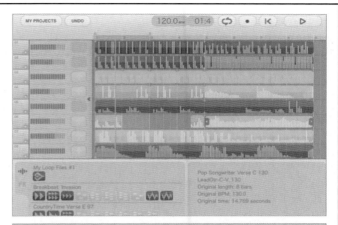

■ Variable note range helps you focus on particular areas

■ Practise in any key within a beautifully designed environment

■ Loops can be layered up to three deep on each track

Price: £1.79/$2.99 **Developer:** Shining Code

Note Goal Pro

Spruce up your sight-reading skills with this excellent training app

A comprehensive sight-reading trainer, Note Goal Pro is aimed at advanced musicians and beginners alike. Turning note identification into a sort of game, complete with a high-score table and fast time bonuses, the main display consists of a piano keyboard set beneath a control panel and faux LCD stave on which notes are displayed. Use the buttons provided to select the key you want to work in, hit the Play button and away you go! Eight random notes will appear on the stave, and you play them on the piano keyboard, the app marking your progress as you go. A clear round of eight notes correctly identified lights up a star, and the next eight notes appear. At the end of the round, the more stars you have, the bigger the bonus score you receive. Entertaining, fun and educational with a classy, modern interface, three help levels, colour coding, resizable keyboard and even a silent mode so you identify notes by sight alone, this is definitely the app for you if you want to improve your sight-reading skills.

Rating ★★★★★

Price: £4.99/$7.99 **Developer:** Sound Trends LLC

studio.HD

Go crazy with loops, add effects and create arrangements

From the creators of the renowned Looptastic HD comes this loop-based eight-track sequencer and mixer. Loops can be stacked on each track up to 3 layers deep, providing a theoretical total of 24 tracks, and you can also record directly onto a track using the iPad's built-in microphone. At the time of writing, only a few example loops are included to get you started, but full access to the Looptastic library of over 900 loops is available via the internet. A quick email to the developers provides an instant response with download links and installation instructions.

Loops automatically conform to the tempo of the current project so they can be auditioned and dragged into the arrangement on the fly. Arranging and mixing is all done on one screen, but solo and pan controls are mysteriously absent, and you keep feeling that there should be another, separate conventional mixer or loop edit page. These limitations aside, the sound quality is excellent and there's no evidence of the timing issues that seem to beleaguer many similar apps.

Rating ★★★★☆

Essential apps

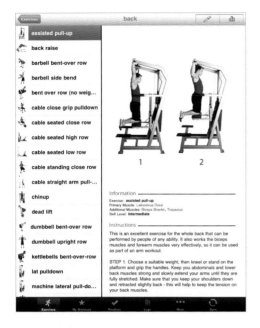

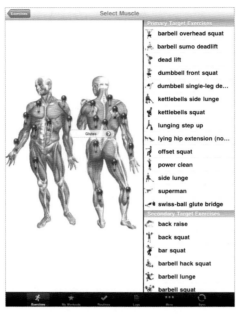

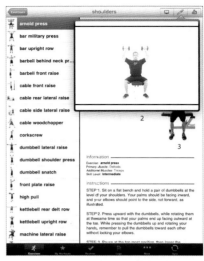

■ If you're not sure on how best to perform an exercise then watch one of the many tutorials

■ You can choose which individual muscles you work out by tapping on this handy chart

Price: £2.99/$4.99   **Developer:** Medical Productions

iFitness HD Bigger and much, much better than ever before

After being highly impressed with the iPhone version of this app, we were keen to see if any improvements had been made to the iPad offering. If you're looking for lots of new additions then prepare to be disappointed because the changes here are largely cosmetic, with the larger iPad screen making great use of showing off the huge amount of exercises and tutorials that are available to you.

What's impressive about iFitness HD is just how comprehensive a package it is. There are over 330 different exercises to choose that cover every muscle group. Exercises for abdominals, shoulders, chest and cardio and all of them are well illustrated and very easy to follow. Further categories enable you to exercise by muscle or equipment and it's also possible to add and create your own to the ever growing list that Medical Productions routinely updates. If you're not sure on whether you're performing exercises correctly there are a number of handy videos available to ensure that you're following things correctly and won't cause yourself an injury.

Once you've become accustomed to all the various exercises and techniques you can start training properly thanks to the handy workout sheets and routines that are included. The routines in particular are very useful, slowly building you up with simple beginner steps that will exercise specific parts of your body. It's also possible to make logs of when you plan to exercise and what your workouts will consist of, ensuring that you never miss a routine.

Other handy additions include a weight monitor, a BMI calculator and the ability to sync with all the iFitness information that's available on your iPhone version. It's all straightforward and easy to use, nicely presented and a testament to the sheer quality that has gone into this impressive app.

It's disappointing that Medical Productions hasn't included a large number of new features, but there's no denying that iFitness remains an incredibly useful app. Download it immediately.

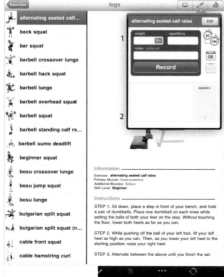

"The 330 different exercises cover every muscle group"

Rating ★★★★★

Price: Free   Developer: BSkyB

Sky Sports News
All the very latest sports news in this app from Sky TV

Sky and its range of sports channels have certainly taken over the sports events and news television airwaves in the past few years, so can they do the same on the iPad? The Sky Sports News application has one main attraction and that is it's completely free. For the princely sum of zero pounds you get an app that keeps you up-to-date with a range of sports news, results and opinion, and it's pretty good too considering this zero price point.

From the outset you might think that this app is aimed more at football fans rather than covering other sports, but that's not to say the Premier League is all that's available. Both codes of rugby, Formula 1, golf and cricket are all included as well as tennis and boxing. If you're looking for other sports, however, you'll be disappointed. This does help to keep the interface nice and simple so you can quickly get to the sports news though. However, don't think that there's not much content, with an average of 12 stories on each sport.

Some of the news stories come with video footage too and it's really very good, enhancing the reporting. Shortly after a Chelsea match ended there was an interview with the manager up and streaming. Sometimes news stories are short, but they are probably about the right length for reading on the iPad.

Subscribers to Sky Mobile TV can also watch the actual Sky Sports News TV feed. Even if you're not a Sky customer in any capacity you get access to Sky Sports Radio within the application. For those of you familiar with the television version of Sky Sports News you'll recognise the news ticker along the bottom of the screen with breaking news and other information. On the right-hand side there are league tables, latest scores and the like.

There's not much in the way of settings, but you can set the order in which each sport appears in the tabs across the top of the screen and the time taken to refresh the app.

If you don't have access to a TV with Sky and you want to keep in touch with what's going on where and when in the world of sport, albeit a small selection of sports, then the Sky Sports News app is great. Keeping an eye on results and upcoming fixtures is a breeze and it's great for catching up on all the big sports stories.

Rating ★★★★★

■ The video clips supplied with the Sky Sports News app are available soon after they are aired on the actual news channel. They add a really great dimension to the app

■ The settings allow you to choose the order of sports and which leagues or competitions are shown in the sidebars

■ Though the selection of alternative sports news isn't all that great, the depth of content for the sports that are covered is very good

Essential apps

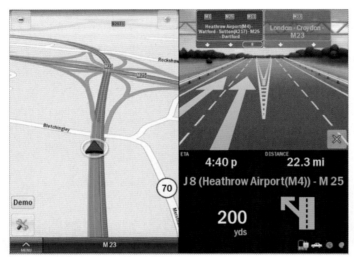

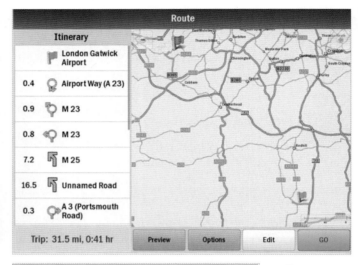

■ There's a split-screen mode with lane guidance

■ Plan your route before you set off

Price: £25.99/$42.99 **Developer:** ALK Technologies Ltd

CoPilot Live HD Europe

Full screen voice-guided GPS navigation for the iPad 3G

Turn-by-turn navigation apps were a brilliant idea on the iPhone, the diminutive form factor and go-anywhere portability of the device lending itself perfectly to the job in hand. The iPad, however, is a completely different animal, much larger and a bit more unwieldy to have in the car while on the move, and the jury is still out as to whether or not it makes as good a solution.

ALK Technologies seem to think it's a viable option, as the developer was among the first of the major players to reveal an iPad-specific version of its successful CoPilot Live voice-guided navigation system. Before we go any further, we feel at pains to point out that this app is only compatible with 3G model iPads – if you have a Wi-Fi-only version, do not buy this.

In many respects, the CoPilot experience on the iPad is actually even more fulfilling. The larger screen displays the information beautifully with pinch-zoom functionality, the split-screen mode the most obvious beneficiary of the increase in screen. The larger memory capacity also means that the more detailed street maps can be stored on the device, so you can still access them when you have no mobile reception.

All of the usual checklist items of mobile satnav features are present and

■ Information looks great displayed on the big screen

correct – postcode lookup, lane indicator display, waypoints, speed camera and speed limit warnings and choice of voices. When you buy the app, you have to choose one European map region to be included as standard, with others being available as subsequent in-app purchases. Live weather and live traffic services are also available to subscribe to via this method.

A recent fix seems to have cured a problem with reported memory issues, and in our tests the app proved to be very reliable. Route directions were clear and accurate, recalculations were swift, and the various voices could all be heard clearly through the iPad speaker. You can also access your iTunes library from within the app, the music volume ducking beneath the voice directions when necessary.

Altogether, we're still not entirely sure it makes any more sense than the iPhone version, but CoPilot Live HD Europe is nonetheless an excellent, well-priced little app that performs its allotted task rather beautifully indeed.

> "The iPad's larger screen displays the information beautifully with pinch-zoom functionality and a split-screen mode"

Rating ★★★★☆

■ Find a restaurant by simply selecting one of three options or tap spin to let Urbanspoon choose for you

■ Find reviews of local restaurants and view a location map and price range on one page

Price: Free **Developer:** Urbanspoon

Urbanspoon

Get ratings and reviews of all the best restaurants wherever you are

Sampling the local cuisine is an essential element of a holiday. Finding a good restaurant can be tricky, though. If your hotel has a friendly doorman then perhaps you can get some advice there, but making the right choices can be tough.

Urbanspoon aims to take the chance out of your eating experience by collecting together simple reviews of all the eating establishments in the area. Urbanspoon will use your iPad's location data to find you or you can select a city yourself. When your location has been determined you have three options: choose price range, style of food and narrow down your location.

Restaurants are shown on a map and you can check to see how many people like the food by tapping on the pin. If you're not really sure what you want you can spin the dials like a fruit machine to have a restaurant chosen for you at random. It's a great way of finding good places to eat when you're on the move.

Rating ★★★★★

■ View all the local interesting visitor attractions on one handy map

■ You can see a general overview of each interesting place within a set distance from your location

Price: Free **Developer:** Stephan Gillmeier

Wikihood for iPad
All the tourist information you need on your iPad

Ever find yourself out of your depth when visiting places far from home? Finding information about a strange place can be a tricky exercise. Searching though endless leaflets or trips to tourist information might be your only option. Well, Wikihood is designed to help you find your feet no matter where you are in the world.

Wikihood locates your position and then does a search to find the most relevant information about the local area. It's restricted to potential tourist-friendly sites, but also includes relevant local information so you'll get a feel for where you are.

Once you've seen something you're interested in all you have to do is tap on it to find out more. A map of where the attraction is and any relevant pictures are displayed to give you a short overview of the place.

Inevitably, some of the information can end up being a touch generic and relies upon the accuracy of information that is available on the internet, but it's generally very good. For a quick overview of the local area Wikihood is a great tool to get you started.

Rating ★★★★★

Essential apps

Price: £5.99/$9.99 **Developer:** Avatron Software

Air Display

Use your iPad as a secondary wireless monitor for your Mac or PC. It works like magic, and you'll soon be wondering how you lived without it

For productive work, having a second monitor makes so much sense. It can be used for tool boxes, secondary apps or for simply controlling iTunes. It's especially useful when using a computer with a small display, such as a MacBook. Air Display takes this idea and applies it to the iPad.

Setting up is easy enough: simply download the app then follow the on-screen instructions to download the software for your Mac or Windows computer. Once installed, you are just a few clicks away from the iPad coming to life and showing your desktop background on its display. Simply move your mouse cursor off the computer screen and it will appear on the iPad. To move windows and programs to the iPad, simply drag them across. Via the System Preferences pane you can tell the computer if the iPad is above, below, to the right or left of it, and by rotating the iPad you can use it in landscape or portrait mode too.

When moving large objects around the screen there's a slight lag to the video; which is to be expected as the signal is sent wirelessly from the desktop computer to the iPad via a router. You wouldn't be able to watch a video on the iPad, but for controlling applications and using the iPad as a secondary display, it works brilliantly. Simply move the mouse cursor however, and it moves in real-time.

Pick up the iPad and you suddenly have a portable monitor for your computer, one that can be passed to others for demonstrations – or showing off. There's also another great feature built into Air Display, and that's the use of Multi-Touch. It's possible to place a window onto the iPad's display, and then use a finger to drag it around the screen. It's not as fluid or intuitive as using a Magic Trackpad, but for basic tasks it's fun and removes the need for using a mouse.

Air Display is a fantastic app that really adds value to an iPad. It also works using an iPhone or iPod touch, although it's not possible to use more than once device at the same time.

Rating ★★★★★

■ Stretch Safari over both your computer and iPad screens

> "Pick up the iPad and you suddenly have a portable monitor for your Mac"

■ Sit the iPad next to your MacBook Pro and you'll have an extended view

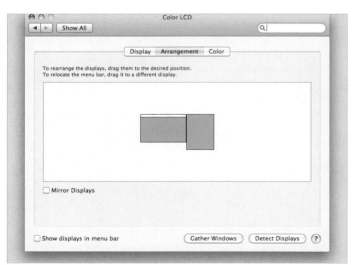
■ Customise the layout of the screens from System Preferences

Price: £3.36/$5.99 Developer: Qrayon, LLC

Air Sketch

Share sketches and notes from your iPad with a HTML 5 browser

This is a really clever and unique app. It comes from the makers of Air Display, and features the same wireless video-based technology. It enables the user to draw on their iPad and display the image live on a desktop computer, iPhone or iPod touch.

To get started, fire up your iPad, open Air Sketch, and then open the specified URL on any HTML 5 compatible browser. That's all you need to do; once set up the image displayed in the browser updates in real-time with the drawing on your iPad. The effect is almost magical, and a great way to quickly sketch or write a message. It's like having a mini whiteboard in your hands.

Some of the app's other great features include Multi-Touch zoom, five drawing tools (pencil, pen, marker, brush and highlighter), a full-colour palette, the ability to save sketches, plus an option for email sketches as PDFs or images. It's intuitive to use and quick to set up. If you're looking for a great way to share sketches and notes with friends and colleagues, then this is it.

Rating ★★★★★

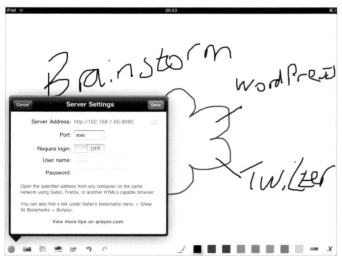

■ Different types of pen and colour options help you categorise notes

■ Turn your iPad into a digital whiteboard

Price: £0.59/$0.99 Developer: Richard Trautvetter

Atomic Web Browser

A mobile browser with some great, desktop class features

Safari on the iPad is a fantastic mobile browser; it's quick, easy to use and provides a great internet experience. However, it's lacking a few key features that hold it back: tabs, a full-screen mode, an ad blocker and advanced Multi-Touch controls. Atomic Web Browsers has all of these features, plus even more.

The addition of tabs make reading multiple pages much easier, enabling the user to switch pages with the tap of a finger and also see how many pages are currently open. The full-screen mode makes websites look even more attractive, and it's possible to emulate desktop browsers to avoid mobile or iPad specific pages. The clever Multi-Touch controls include two-finger swipes to switch tabs, close tabs, and load the homepage. A three-finger tap enables the user to enter or exit full screen mode. Atomic Web Browser also uses the same WebKit rendering engine as Safari and its desktop brother, so browsing webpages is just as smooth and quick. With the high number of unique features built into this app, it's an essential download.

Rating ★★★★★

■ The settings pane is packed with options

■ Finally, tabs on an iPad browser!

Price: £2.99/$4.99 **Developer:** Catamount Software

PocketMoney

Take control of your finances with a friendly account system

Modern life is both expensive and financially complex, so keeping track of your accounts, especially in this economic climate, is very important. However, budgeting and keep track of your transactions is not the most fun way to pass your time if you're prone to bury your head in the sand and live payday to payday.

Enter the world of PocketMoney, which can be run as a simple tracker for your current account, or it can look after a variety of account types and link them all together to let you know exactly how much cash you have or how deep a hole you're in. The initial set up will take some time, but is so worth it. The first step is to define each account type – cash, checkbook, credit card, online etc and enter the regular income and outgoings, such as salaries and direct debits. The frequency of these can be set to daily, weekly, monthly or annually. Unfortunately this misses out money that may be paid bi-weekly or every four weeks. It's these type of payments that are the hardest to track as they shift through the calendar, and as such it's a trick PocketMoney has missed.

The other main function, that of budgets, has a bi-weekly option, and while there is clear duplication of function here, it's useful because it allows specific targets to be set and tracked. See how much you spend per year on your morning latte!

Each transaction can be categorised so that various search functions and filters can be applied to show types of transaction, which is handy if you are looking for something. An autocomplete feature also helps entering transactions – which are broken down into deposit, withdraw and transfer – as easy as possible. There are add-ons to the program that allow for charts and graphics and also photo-receipts to be tagged to transactions. The overall aim is to show you the cashflow through the month so you can both track your expenditure and assets.

For the casual user, this is all they really need to track their money, but for the would-be accountant, reporting is also available. Synching is offered in numerous ways, from down the cable to browser FTP and also Wi-Fi. There are also related apps from Catamount that work well with PocketMoney, such as MPG, CheckPlease and BillMinder. The app supports import and export of TDF, CSV and QIF file formats (and import of OFX), though there have been some complaints over the accuracy of the QIF exporting. The bottom line is if you want to keep an eye on both your day-to-day accounts and also any secondary and investments then this is a great budget app to do it.

Rating ★★★★☆

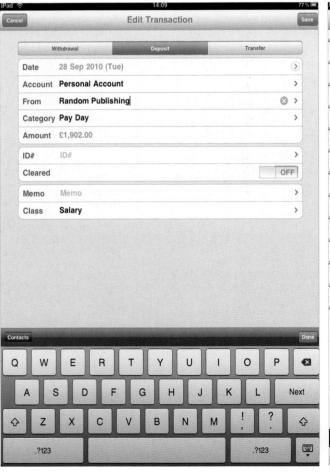

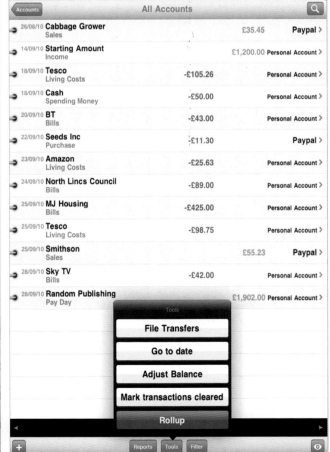

■ (Right) Get an overall view of all activity on all accounts. Then tweak individual entries or accounts

■ (Left) Defining regular deposits and withdrawals is painless and they can then be set to repeat

Price: Free   Developer: iHandySoft Inc.

Alarm Clock HD Free

Always make sure you're on time with this iPad alarm clock

Whatever the reason for the decision, the fact remains that the iPad doesn't have an alarm clock, but it does seem like a strange choice by Apple to leave off what's such a simple tool. However, this has left the way open for independent developers to bridge the gap, and there are plenty on offer on the App Store.

Alarm Clock HD displays a nice large digital clock in a pleasant green shade. The brightness of the clock can be adjusted with a simple pinch. You can show extra information such as the day of the week, weather and display the time in 24 or 12-hour formats. In addition, the app will show you a basic local weather forecast and displays which city you're in, should you forget.

Setting an alarm is easy and you can decide upon a number of factors to suit your needs. Snooze options can be set anywhere from 2 minutes to 30 minutes or never if you always spritely enough to jump out of bed the moment you're woken. The volume of the alarm is editable and you can have it fade in rather than just go of at full volume if you prefer. There are nine sounds to choose from and you can set as many alarms throughout the day as you choose.

Of course, multitasking isn't supported on iPads running versions before OS 4.2, so you have to ensure that the alarm clock is running for those alarms to go off. Remember to set it before you go to bed though and you'll be fine. Those with OS 4.2 or later should be good to go as you can set your alarms and leave them without having to worry.

There's a paid-for version of Alarm Clock HD that adds a variety of colour themes and allows you to use the iPad as a flashlight. Perhaps the most appealing aspect of the paid-for app is the ability to wake up to the music on your iPad as opposed to an alarm signal. It costs just £1.19 ($1.99) to unlock the extra functionality.

Alarm Clock HD is great if all you need is a simple alarm clock and time display, and the addition of local weather to the display is a nice touch if you're too tired to head over to the window and open the curtains. It's got enough options to suit most needs and the ability to set repeats and snooze options is welcome. Obviously, having to remember to leave it as the last app running is a bit of a pain, but that's solved by upgrading to OS 4.2.

Rating ★★★★★

■ See the time, day of the week and a basic weather forecast for where you are in the world

■ Set up multiple alarms with a variety of sounds and show or hide the fine details on screen

■ You can upgrade the app to take advantage of your music collection and further colour options

Essential apps

Price: £5.99/$9.99 **Developer:** SHAPE Services

IM+ Pro

Why have multiple apps for communicating with friends, when you can have just the one?

It may have a high asking price, but IM+ Pro is packed with features that make communicating over the web a breeze. It supports every major chat program available, so that's GTalk, MSN/Live, AIM/iChat, ICQ, MySpace, Twitter, Facebook, Jabber and Skype. When the app is opened it displays every chat service in a pop-up window. There's no pre-registration required, so it's case of choosing a service and logging in with the username and password.

Using each chat service is a breeze, and once added any relevant contacts are added to the apps contacts bar. Twitter also adds timelines, favourites, nearby, followers and following.

Part of the app's high asking price can be explained by the availability of push notifications for each service. Even if IM+ Pro is closed, when a new message is available a pop-up window appears on the iPad's screen to alert the user. IM+ Pro will display push notifications for each service for seven days after the app is closed, with one exception: notifications from Skype only appear for two hours after the app is closed.

A handful of further additions contribute to the app. A built-in web browser means web links in conversations can be viewed from within the app. Users can enable custom sounds for incoming messages, contacts becoming available and push alerts. A range of animated emoticons are included for use within messages, and the app enables users to customise its appearance by importing background wallpapers from the Photo Library. This latter feature makes the experience more personal, although complex images can distract from content. The user interface is perhaps the only negative aspect to the app. It has a cluttered feel, and with the use of pop-up windows for accessing settings and accounts you can't help but wish for a more streamlined approach. Nevertheless,

this is a fantastic app for those who enjoy chatting online. It bundles every major chat service into one app that's easy to use and packed with features. For those who don't use Skype or wish for Push Notifications, then a free version of the app titled IM+ Lite is also available from the App Store.

Rating ★★★★★

■ Check out new Tweets from within the app

■ Speech recognition can be enabled via an in-app purchase

■ The Lite version includes most web-communication services

■ Plenty of options are available when posting a tweet

■ See user details at the tap of a finger

Price: £2.99/$4.99 **Developer:** Dev

Tweets

A Twitter client with geo location controls and more

The official Twitter app is rather special, with its futuristic tab-based interface that makes reading and writing tweets a breeze. So it takes something unique to make an app to stand out from the crowd. Tweets attempts to grab attention by focusing on three unique areas: GeoAnywhere, which enables users to post their Current Location or make one up using Google Maps, StreamingTweets, which automatically breaks up long tweets into 140 character chunks and organises them in a timeline, and Emoticons, with 470 icons to choose from.

The app also includes TweetSecrets, a rather clever touch that enables users to post a private tweet that can only be read using a code key, as well as the usual Twitter features one would expect.

In all, this is a clever app with some unique touches. It does have a few niggling problems, however. Due to the user interface design the app works best in portrait mode (in landscape mode the post option buttons are annoyingly hidden by the keyboard), and it also has a chrome notebook appearance which some might find unattractive.

Rating ★★★★☆

■ Swap between the mobile and full versions of Facebook with a 3D effect

Price: £0.59/$0.99 **Developer:** eFUSION

Dual Viewer For Facebook

A must for regular FB users

Accessing the full features of Facebook on your iPad can be quite a chore. The mobile version of the site works great when it comes to accessibility and controls, but it doesn't support video playback found when visiting the full website in Safari. Dual Viewer For Facebook works around this problem in a clever way: it includes two versions of the site that can be switched between at the tap of a finger, with a 3D turning effect that echoes the iBooks store. As a result, this is an efficient way to access Facebook on your iPad.

As expected the app includes every feature you would need when accessing Facebook. In mobile mode the user can update their status, check in at places, comment and like posts, plan and join events, see friends and access the inbox. The full version of the site also includes video playback, adverts, pokes and requests.

The ability to instantly swap between the two versions of Facebook is a clever and novel approach. For those who regularly use Facebook, this is a highly recommended app.

Rating ★★★★★

Essential apps

■ The home screen is reasonably tidy, but what have you done with Pluto?

■ Check out the progress of on-going missions with plenty of facts and attractive graphics

Price: Free **Developer:** NASA Ames Research

NASA App

Explore the universe with experts

The iPad is well served for astronomy because as well as Star Walk there's the official NASA app. Starting with a home screen showing the solar system, though not Pluto, which could have been included if only for the 'is it or isn't it a planet' debate.

Anyway, tap on one of these to get a pile of information, far more than Star Walk. Linked into these you can also check out missions that are ongoing like the Cassini probe and the ISS. Also on the homepage are links to newly uploaded pictures from the agency, featured stories and video from either the collection that's stored on YouTube or from NASA TV.

Once you get off the main screen and into the featured areas the presentation dips, the usability suffers and it becomes an exercise in wading through the information. There are also a great deal of the photographs not stored in the app; they are on the NASA website instead, so an internet connection is required to pull them in. Obviously it helps with the app size but again, makes it slower. Not a bad effort from the rocket scientists, but it really does need better organisation.

Rating ★★★☆☆

■ The timed element enables students to compete against each other, even if the questions are fairly easy

Price: £2.39/$3.99 **Developer:** Paul Schmitt

MathBoard

Competitive counting makes maths more fun. Honestly!

The prospect of practising maths is one to fill any student with dread, especially the younger age range that this app is aimed at. It offers addition, subtraction, multiplication, division, squares, cube and square roots. Okay, here's the clever stuff: you can have questions up as a quiz, both timed and untimed, or as problems to be solved. The answers can be set so that the user has to enter them, or select from multiple choice answers.

It's all presented on an old-school style chalkboard format, and you have enough space on the board to do your workings out. The quizzes can be saved so you can test different students later and the scope of the questions is completely configurable from the number, to the range of variables and type of mathematic problem. Getting kids to complete the quizzes in the fastest time certainly introduces an element of competition that makes learning more fun, but whether the option to have an expiring clock to race against is a slightly more cruel way to get them to learn we're not sure.

Rating ★★★★☆

■ The app also includes a brief overview of the entire world

Price: £1.19/$1.99 **Developer:** Fuzzy Peach LLC

The World Factbook for iPad

All you'll ever need to know about the world's countries in one app

Updated every two weeks with new facts and figures, this app presents detailed and thorough information on more than 250 countries and locations throughout the world. Each listing includes an introduction, flag with description, colour map, location map, geographic coordinates, statistics on its people, government, economy, military, current issues and more. By digging further into the app users will find options to compare countries, including imports and exports, communication systems and transportation.

In landscape mode every country and location appears in a list with its flag on the left of the screen. In portrait mode the list can be accessed via a button in the top-left corner. When viewing a location it's possible to access nine overall subjects using buttons at the top of the screen. There's a wealth of information to be found in this app. The data presented is almost endless, and a continued source of inspiration. It's the perfect app for anyone with an interest in the wider world, students or those who travel to a number of varied locations. Best of all, the app works offline as all the information is stored within the app.

Rating ★★★★★

■ See six words of the day. Shake the iPad to see more

Price: £1.99/$2.99 **Developer:** TranCreative Software

WordBook XL

The entire English dictionary, thesaurus and more in one app

A combination of both dictionary and thesaurus, WorldBook XL has been the top-selling commercial English dictionary app since its release in 2008. For good reason too – it's easy to use and packed with clever features.

When opened in landscape the app presents a search bar on the left of the screen with a results window on the right. In portrait mode the search bar can be accessed via a button in the top-left corner. Searching happens in real time, so as the user types a word the results appear below as they type. The default result is taken from the English dictionary, with nouns, adverbs and adjectives present. At the top of the results window are buttons for displaying any links to further words, a thesaurus link and three buttons that display result content from Wikipedia, answers.com and Google. It's possible to bookmark results for later reference, learn phonetics in IPA, AHD and M-W systems, create and edit notes and see words of the day that can be randomised with a shake of the iPad.

Rating ★★★★★

All your questions answered in these simple and straightforward tips and advice

Your problems solved

Put your worries aside as we fix your difficulties right here

168   Can't connect to Wi-Fi
Recharging via USB
Turning the iPad off
Charging the iPad

169   Frozen iPad
3G problems
Exporting documents
Unresponsive screen
How to take a screenshot
Delete apps
Read your emails
Reorganise the Home screens

170   Backing up forever
Keep your iPad awake
Multitasking woes
Syncing Outlook Mail,
Calendar and Contacts

171   iPad not recognised
Add a signature to emails
Lock your iPad
Different fonts
Become a picture frame

172   Top ten tips for saving your
battery power

> "Don't worry, the chances of your iPad being broken are actually very slim"

Top pick
Connect to Wi-Fi

Top pick
Charging fixes

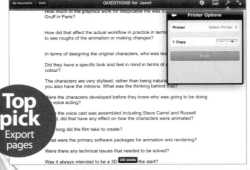

Top pick
Export pages

Top pick
Take a screenshot

ing

"The beauty of the iPad is that you can put it into standby mode and it uses very little power"

Troubleshooting

Your problems solved

If you have trouble with any aspect of using your iPad then you've come to the right place. Pull up a seat and let's sort it out

Can't connect to Wi-Fi

I can't seem to be able to connect my iPad to my home Wi-Fi signal or ones at hot spots in cafes and places like that. Is my iPad broken?
Robert Dunbar

A There are lots of reasons why the iPad can't pick up a signal or connect to a Wi-Fi service, but some of those are outside the remit of this magazine as they are highly technical. The simpler solutions are that firstly, Wi-Fi might be turned off. Tap on the Settings app and tap on 'Wi-Fi'. If it is turned off then there is a slider to move to turn it back on. The next reason is that the iPad might be able to find the Wi-Fi network, but if it is secured – and your home network should be – then you will need to enter the network key (the password) for it. Firstly, select the right network from the ones listed under 'Choose a Network…' Tap on it. If it requires a network key it will immediately ask you for it. This is the password that your

home network uses. Type it in exactly and it should now connect. Cafes that have free Wi-Fi still often use passwords, but the process can be slightly different. Follow the same procedure by going to Wi-Fi and selecting the network you want. You will now join the network. If it's completely unrestricted, that will be all you have to do. If it requires a password then normally this is accessed through a web browser. It should automatically load Safari and take you to the homepage where the password can be entered. If it doesn't, then try tapping on Safari and running it yourself.

The other reasons for lack of Wi-Fi connectivity can simply be that you are too far away from the signal or that the signal is being interfered with by other equipment. If you have a wireless handset phone located next to the Wi-Fi router, for example, it can interfere with it. Try moving it or the router somewhere else.

■ If you are having problems connecting to a Wi-Fi network, check to make sure that it is actually there!

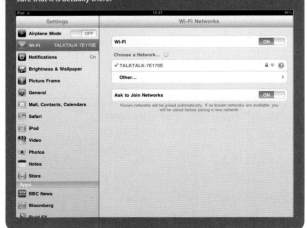

Recharging via USB

I've plugged my iPad into the USB lead and connected it to my computer, but it never seems to charge. Unlike, for example, if I plug my iPhone into it.
David Toms

A The simple answer is that no, it might not do. The charge available through USB isn't high and the iPad demands a lot of juice to recharge. That's why the iPad comes with a mains charger. For fast recharging, you should use that instead. When the iPad is connected to a computer it can recharge, but not usually if the iPad is on, or even if it is in standby and you have a lot apps running that use notifications, because they will still secretly check for alerts. To give your iPad the best chance to recharge through the USB lead, either make sure that no apps are running and none are in suspend mode through multitasking. See the question further on about multitasking. To give your iPad the best chance of recharging, turn it off completely – see the next question.

Turning the iPad off

Normally I just press the little black button at the top of the iPad to turn it off, but I notice that the battery has

gone down slightly the next time I turn it on again. A friend of mine said that it was just in standby mode and not actually off, so how do I really turn it off?
Emma Gillespie

A The beauty of the iPad is that you can put it into standby mode and it uses very little power. When you want to use it, one press of a button instantly brings it on. However, it does still use some power when in standby mode, especially if you have lots of apps multitasking. To turn your iPad off completely, press and hold down the on/off button on the top right until the screen goes black and a red bar with the words "Slide to power off" appears. Slide the bar across to power down the iPad or tap Cancel to go back. When you turn it on again it will take approximately 30 seconds to power back up. Incidentally, the button on the top is called both the on/off button and also the sleep/wake button, depending on which action you are actually doing.

Charging the iPad

I am using the power charger for the iPad but it takes ages for it to recharge. Is there any way of speeding the process up?
Lora Allen

■ If you have lots of apps running at the same time, then charging via the USB lead is nigh on impossible

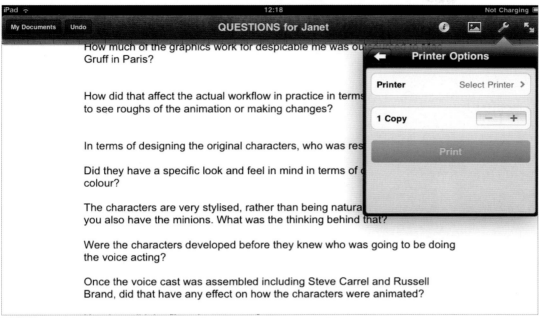

iPad 📶   12:18   Not Charging ▣

| My Documents | Undo | **QUESTIONS for Janet** | ⓘ   ▣   🔧   ⤢ |

How much of the graphics work for despicable me was ou̶t̶s̶o̶u̶r̶c̶e̶d̶ ̶t̶o̶ ̶M̶a̶c̶
Gruff in Paris?

How did that affect the actual workflow in practice in terms
to see roughs of the animation or making changes?

In terms of designing the original characters, who was res̶

Did they have a specific look and feel in mind in terms of c̶
colour?

The characters are very stylised, rather than being natura̶l̶
you also have the minions. What was the thinking behind that?

Were the characters developed before they knew who was going to be doing
the voice acting?

Once the voice cast was assembled including Steve Carrel and Russell
Brand, did that have any effect on how the characters were animated?

Printer Options

| Printer | Select Printer ❯ |
| 1 Copy | −   + |

Print

■ With the new version of the operating system you now have more ways to export your work documents

"It's very rare for the iPad to completely freeze, but it can still happen"

A *Normally, the mains power charger will recharge the iPad fairly quickly, but if it's taking a long time it's probably because you have a lot of apps running at once. So the solution is just the same as if recharging using the USB lead. If you ensure that no apps are running in the background then it should recharge quickly, even on standby mode. If you turn the iPad off completely it will recharge very quickly.*

Frozen iPad
My iPad has completely locked up. The Home button and the on/off button don't do anything and the screen is frozen and unresponsive. Please help!
Jamie Bradforth

A *The iPad may run a mobile operating system but it's still a computer and computers do occasionally crash. It's very rare for the iPad to completely freeze, but it can still happen. In this case press the Home button and the on/off button together for 10 seconds. The iPad should then reset itself.*

3G problems
I have recently bought an iPad on eBay that has 3G mode built in but I can't seem to get it to work! Is there anything I should be doing with the iPad to activate it?
Dennis Hartland

A *There are two things about the 3G reception. The first is that your iPad needs to have a microSim installed that allows for a data package to be paid for. Without one, you can't access the 3G network. Numerous mobile network vendors offer packages based on how much information you access over the 3G network and bill you every month. So, you need the microSim and a data plan package. The other thing is that reception can be variable depending on where you are, so some more remote areas of the country don't have any 3G coverage at all, while others are rated only for reception outside buildings, not indoors. It's worth checking the coverage maps by each vendor to make sure the areas important to you are fully covered. See page 35 for how to set up your iPad for 3G.*

Exporting documents
I use Pages and Numbers a lot, but it's a bit of pain to export documents through iTunes all the time. What else can I do to export them?
Aimee Donovan

A *Firstly, with iOS 4.2 you can now print directly to wireless printers, so there's no need to export to do that. Tap on the Tools icon to select Print (see p118 for more). If you go back out of a document to the general documents view there are also options to email the document, share via iWork.com or use cloud storage services like iDisk or a specific web server using WebDAV.*

Unresponsive screen
My iPad was working okay, but recently the screen become unresponsive and sometimes things slow right down and then speed right up again making it pretty much unusable. What do you think is causing this and how do I fix it?
Petr Jaroslaw

A *The quick answer is to reset the iPad. See the 'Frozen iPad' question on this page to find out how to do it. If that doesn't fix the problem then it's likely to be a hardware fault. Take the iPad into your nearest Apple store and if it's under warranty then you can have it exchanged.*

Top tips

Take a screenshot

If you want to take a screenshot of whatever is on the screen at that moment, press the on/off button and the Home button at the same time. The screen grab will be saved in your Photos folder under Saved Photos. It can be emailed, printed or transferred via USB.

Delete apps
Tap and hold on an icon for any app until all the apps start to wobble. A cross also appears in the corner of each one. Tap this to call up the Delete dialogue box and then tap 'Delete'.

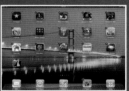

Read those mails?
Delete old emails by swiping your finger over them from right to left. The word Delete will appear. Tap on this to remove it. See page 52 for more on emails.

Reorganise the Home screens
Tap and hold the icon for an app until the screen goes into wobble mode. Now, keep holding and move the icon around the screen. Release to drop into place.

Backing up forever

Whenever I come to back up my iPad by connecting it to iTunes through the computer, it seems to take an absolute age to do it. How can I make it do this much quicker?

Michel Ronstat

A *If you were using an iPhone the answer would probably lie with the number of pictures you had on the camera roll, but in the case of the iPad, it's more likely to be a dodgy app – there's no real reason with iOS 4.2 for it to be particularly slow.*

So, cancel the backup and, in iTunes, click on the entry for your iPad in the pane on the left side of the window. Now click on the Apps tab that appears above the central area of iTunes. There's an option to Sync Apps, which will have a tick in it. Click on this to remove the tick. Now try the backup. If it goes quickly then it was indeed a bad app. Now, put the tick back into Sync Apps but untick each app individually. Then, starting with the top one, put a tick in the first app and try the sync. If it works fine, put a tick into the next app and try again. Keep going through the apps until you get to one where the backup now takes forever. That's your bad app.

To fix the app, you should check to see if there is an update available for it. Click on Apps under the Library heading on the left side pane. On the bottom-right corner it will tell you if there are any updates for the app currently available. Click on this text or the right-facing arrow to go to the updates page. Is your app listed here? Even if it's not, we recommend that you keep all your apps updated anyway, so click on either Get Update for the individual app, or Download All to update everything.

Do another sync and, if it backs up properly, all is now fine. If it doesn't then it looks like the app is corrupt. Click on the Apps entry under Library again and then right-click on the app in question. From the dialogue box that appears, select 'Delete'. Remove the app from iTunes. Now, is the app working fine on the iPad itself? If so, then go ahead and sync and agree to the option that comes up to copy back to iTunes. This should put the good version of the app back into iTunes. If the app doesn't actually work on your iPad, then either delete it from the iPad first or, when doing the sync, decline the option to transfer back to iTunes as this will remove it from the iPad as well.

"If the app doesn't work on your iPad, then either delete it from the iPad first or, when doing the sync, decline the option to transfer back to iTunes"

■ The key to finding bad apps is to untick Sync Apps and try them out one at a time

Feeling sleepy?

My iPad keeps turning itself off really quickly to the extent that I am perpetually having to switch it back on. This is really annoying because I do like to browse things while chatting and then I find that it's gone to sleep. Aside from coffee, how do you make it stay awake?

Sophie Lucas

A *This is precisely the opposite of one of the battery-saving tip ideas seen on page 173. You either like the timed sleep mode or it gets on your nerves. If you don't mind using power like there's no tomorrow go to the Settings app and tap on General. Tap on Auto-Lock and tap on 15 Minutes or Never.*

Multitasking woes

Some of my apps keep saying that memory is running low and I should close other apps that are open. I know that multitasking is now supported but I don't know how the other apps are running or how to close them.

Garrima Kaul

A *To see what apps are running under multitasking mode press the Home button twice, very quickly. The apps on the main screen fade and a panel will appear at the bottom of the screen showing the apps currently running. Tap and hold on any of them until they all start to wiggle and a red dash appears on the left corner of each icon. Tap the dash to close the apps so that the only one running is the one you are using.*

Syncing Outlook Mail, Calender and Contacts

I have Microsoft Outlook on my computer and want to be able to get my mail, contacts and calendars on my iPad. How do I do it?

Thomas Samuelson

A *Plug your iPad in to the computer so that iTunes recognises it. Click on the name of your iPad under Devices in the left side panel. Then click on the Info tab above the main screen. There are entries for Sync Contacts, Sync Calendars and Sync Mail Accounts. Put a tick in each tickbox and ensure that Outlook is the program selected to sync with. Then click on Sync in the bottom right corner. See page 26 for more information on syncing contacts.*

Tapping the Home button twice will bring up the apps that are currently multitasking

"Tap the dash to close the apps so that the only one running is the one you are using"

The ability to easily synchronise email, contacts and calendars with Outlook is a great feature of the iDevice

Not recognised

My iPad is no longer recognised by my computer. When I plug it in nothing appears under the Devices entry in iTunes. Please help, I'm afraid that my iPad may be broken!
Kaylee Hollick

A Don't worry, the chances of your iPad being broken are very slim. Now there are some very technical causes for this kind of thing happening, but the two most common answers are that either the USB port you are plugging the iPad into is faulty or that iTunes has become corrupt. Try plugging the iPad into a different USB port. If that doesn't work, uninstall iTunes, download the latest version and re-install it. Then try it. There's also a high chance that neither your computer nor your device are faulty. Instead, you may simply have a defective USB cable. If you have another lying around you should try connecting your iPad with that. If nothing works, you should try turning both iPad and computer off and on again; you'd be surprised how many problems that solves!

Top tips

Add a signature

Personalise your emails by adding a signature. Tap on Settings then go to Mail, Contacts, Calendars. Look down the list on the right for Signature. Tap this to enter your message.

Restrict your iPad

Go to the Settings app and tap on General and then on Restrictions. On the new page tap on Enable Restrictions, which requires a four-digit passcode to be set up.

Different fonts

If you use Notes to keep, well, notes, then check out the two new fonts you can use courtesy of iOS 4.2. Go to Settings, then Notes to select them.

Become a picture frame

Turn your iPad into a picture frame by going to Settings then Picture Frame. When you turn your iPad on, instead of swiping to unlock, tap on the Picture Frame icon (see p78 for more).

Top ten tips for saving battery power

The iPad might be able to go all day, but the battery still runs out. Here's how to maximise what power you have

01 Turn it off at night
Not standby, but actually off. You aren't using it but the apps can be so shut it down. Hold down the on/off button until prompted.

02 Turn off Wi-Fi
If you are not using the internet and don't anticipate doing so then turn the Wi-Fi signal off. Tap on Settings and slide Airplane mode to on to turn off all wireless functions.

03 Turn down brightness
How bright the display is affects power usage. The brighter it is, the more power it uses. Tap on the Settings app and then tap on Brightness & Wallpaper. There's a slider that sets how bright the display is. Tap and hold then slide to the left to reduce it.

04 Location services
The iPad has something called 'Location Services' that enables apps to discover where you are. They use the Wi-Fi or 3G signal to do this, which uses power. If you want to squeeze a bit more power out of the battery, turn this feature off by going to the Settings app and tapping on General. Tap on Location Services and either toggle individual apps off or turn the entire service off.

05 Push and Fetch
These are two services that your Mail, Contacts and Calendars use. If you allow the apps to keep checking for new mail or information they can use up battery power. Push

is where new information, such as new email, is sent from the server to your iPad, so your device gets it as soon as it is on the system. It's certainly useful if you really need it, but it drains the battery. So, in Settings, tap on Mail, Contacts, Calendars and tap again on Fetch New Data. There is an entry for Push, so use the slider to set it to Off.

06 Push off
As explained, Fetch is a scheduled service where the iPad goes to the server and checks to see if there is any mail. This can be as often as every 15 minutes. Now, if you are using Push you don't need Fetch, so tap on Manual. Also, if you've set Push to Off, to save battery power set Fetch to Manual as well. Now nothing will be checked unless you run those apps and manually check for new info.

> ## "Slide Airplane mode to on to turn off all wireless functions"

■ The brightness of the screen affects how much power the iPad uses. Turn it down to make the battery last longer

■ While a valuable service to use, you may not want all your apps to be constantly demanding to know where you are

■ Unless you are using Bluetooth accessories like a keyboard then there's no need for it to be on

■ Push notifications send mail and other information from the server when it arrives. Turn it off and check manually when needed

"If you aren't using the iPad but it's still on, it's using up valuable power"

07 Sleep

Let your iPad go into sleep mode more quickly. If you aren't using the iPad but it's still on, then it's using up valuable power needlessly. Let it go into sleep mode more quickly by tapping firstly on Settings then on General. Tap on Auto-Lock and change the time to 2 minutes. If you value your battery life, we recommend you don't have it set to 'Never'.

08 Don't multitask

Don't leave any apps running in multitask mode. Close down the ones that you aren't using. It may take a little bit of getting used to, but your battery life will drastically improve. See the earlier question called 'Multitasking woes' for more details.

09 No Bluetooth unless necessary

Unless you have to use connected external devices like a keyboard, there is no need for Bluetooth to be turned on; having it on with nothing connected still wastes battery life. Go into Settings and tap on Bluetooth, then slide the switch so that it's off.

10 Keep out of the hot and cold

Surprisingly, extremes of temperature will significantly affect your iPad's battery life and performance. Don't leave your device in the car overnight or on a table in the sun.

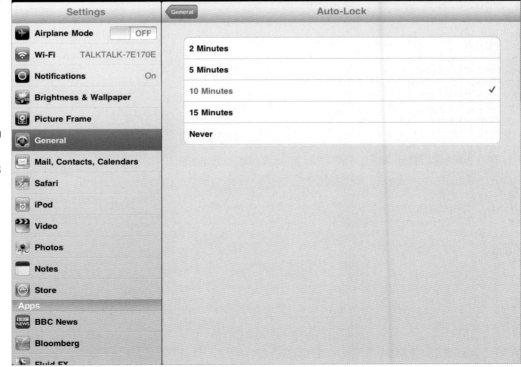

■ The time it takes before your iPad goes into sleep mode can be adjusted so that it happens more quickly

Go creative with Mac, iPad & iPho

Upskill today with the very best creative bookazines and DVDs

Mac for Beginners vol 3

Starting with the basics, this essential guide will teach you how to get to grips with every aspect of your Mac, from iLife and iWork to iTunes, Safari and Mail.

SRP: £12.99

The iPhone Book

This latest revised edition of The iPhone Book brings you a wealth of guides to help you get more out of your smartphone, from getting started to the must-have apps.

SRP: £9.99

iPad 2 App Directory

With 859 reviews covering every section of the App Store, this Directory points you towards the very best apps and games out there for iPad and iPad 2.

SRP: £9.99

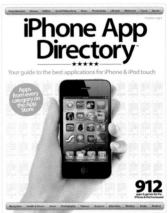

iPhone App Directory vol 8

The world's best iPhone applications are reviewed right here, including the very best for iPhone 4, with every App Store category featured inside.

SRP: £9.99

iPad Tips, Tricks, Apps & Hacks vol 2

Step-by-step tutorials covering the secrets of the iPad and the ultimate jailbreaking guide make this a must-own book.

SRP: £9.99

iPhone Games Directory vol 2

The world's most comprehensive guide to iPhone, iPod touch and iPad gaming apps, with all gaming genres reviewed and rated.

SRP: £9.99

iPhone for Beginners

Everything you need to get started on your iPhone. With step-by-step tutorials and a troubleshooting guide, this is a must-have for iPhone owners .

SRP: £9.99

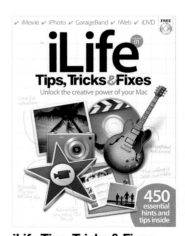

iLife Tips, Tricks & Fixes

Learn to master the complete suite of Apple iLife apps including iPhoto, GarageBand, iMovie, iWeb and iDVD with these in-depth features and guides.

SRP: £12.99

your
ne

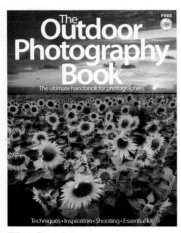

The Outdoor Photography Book
With fantastic shooting ideas to a wide variety of practical tips, this is the only resource for shooting the great outdoors.
SRP: £12.99

Mac for Beginners vol 3
Starting with the basics, this guide will walk you through OS X, iLife, iWork and more. There's also a guide to the best apps to download for your Mac.
SRP: £12.99

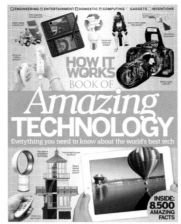

How It Works Book of Amazing Technology
Taking a look into the workings of some of the hottest gadgets and everyday appliances, this is the perfect guide for all tech-lovers.
SRP: £9.99

iPhone App Directory vol 8
The world's best iPhone applications are reviewed right here, including the very best for iPhone 4, with every App Store category featured inside.
SRP: £9.99

The world's best creative bookazines to collect and keep or give as a gift

IMAGINE PUBLISHING

The iPad Book vol 2
The ultimate guide to iPad and iPad 2, this book brings you a wealth of productivity, entertainment and lifestyle tips, with all the top apps to download.
SRP: £9.99

Retro Gamer Collection 5
An unmissable selection of articles featuring timeless games and hardware. From Zelda to Asteroids, this book covers all the classic games from days gone by.
SRP: £9.99

Android for Beginners
If you're new to the Android revolution, this is the book for you. With features and guides suitable for all devices, this book will teach you everything you need to know.
SRP: £9.99

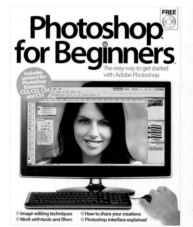

Photoshop for Beginners
Full of great tutorials to help you get to grips with all the tools and techniques of Photoshop, this book will guide you through from the very beginning.
SRP: £12.99

Order online www.imaginebookshop.co.uk

Prices may vary, stocks are limited and shipping prices vary depending on destination